ALSO BY JOYCE REISER KORNBLATT

Nothing to Do with Love, Stories 1981
White Water

Joyce Reiser Kornblatt

A William Abrahams Book

E. P. DUTTON   NEW YORK

Portions of this book were first published as "History's Child" in *Iowa Review*, "Blue Earth" in *Crosscurrents*, and "Offerings" in *Georgia Review*. "Offerings" has since been included in *Prize Stories 1986: The O. Henry Awards*.

Published in the United States by
E. P. Dutton, a division of New American Library,
2 Park Avenue, New York, N.Y. 10016.

Library of Congress Cataloging-in-Publication Data
Kornblatt, Joyce Reiser.
Breaking bread.
"A William Abrahams book."
I. Title.
PS3561.0662B7   1987   813'.54   86-16674
ISBN: 0-525-24388-7

Published simultaneously in Canada by
Fitzhenry & Whiteside Limited, Toronto

COBE

10 9 8 7 6 5 4 3 2 1
First Edition

FOR JEAN LEVA

"Through art, we are able to break bread with the dead, and without communion with the dead a fully human life is impossible."

—W. H. AUDEN

I wish to thank the National Endowment for the Arts for its support during the writing of this book.

Contents

I

Pa

1

On Sunday mornings, my mother tells me, my grandfather went to the Quincy Street pool and swam in the nude.

My grandmother held this against him. It was not her sole complaint. Against her husband, she had two categories of grievances: bad habits and failures. Swimming in the nude was a bad habit, as were sleepwalking and cluttering. To the latter two, Pa took exception. He said he did not sleepwalk; he said he needed solitude and the middle of the night was the only time he could have it. He said the only walking he did was from the bedroom to the kitchen, where he sat at the table and drank a cup

3

of Postum and studied the moon, the constellations. He told her that what she called clutter he considered supplies: wood scraps, newspapers, string, jars, cracker boxes.

Didn't he make his baby girls alphabet blocks from pieces of pine left over from the trestle table he built? Didn't he use the cracker boxes to start seedlings for the garden he grew each summer on the front porch of their second-floor flat, redwood planters brimming with marigolds and pansies, morning glories climbing the string trellises he strung between the porch posts? Didn't he wind up using all those newspapers to cover the broadloom when he painted the parlor's twelve-foot-high walls?

No matter. Clutter was clutter. Sleepwalking was sleepwalking. My grandmother recorded them under bad habits, and there were no erasures in her emotional ledger.

In the failures column, she entered "lack of ambition." My grandfather was the storekeeper, but his wife was the one in the family who kept the accounts.

His business was secondhand clothing.

"Rags," my grandmother said. "Who can make a living from rags?"

"We do all right," Pa said. "We get along."

She wanted jewelry. She wanted to buy three yards of silk and take it to the dressmaker, who would turn it into a tunic with stylish padded shoulders and bound buttonholes and a tasseled sash. She wanted to buy her shoes in Filene's Shoe Salon on the third floor instead of in the bargain basement, where everything smelled musty and looked dull, even the patent leather, as if a fine rain of dust fell constantly on the discounted merchandise.

She wanted a piano, too, a baby grand. In Lithuania, she'd had a baby grand and lessons once a week from Malke Weiss, who had trained at the conservatory at Minsk and claimed to have once met Stokowski.

"Did I come to America to lose everything I had?" my grandmother wailed.

4

"You came like we all did," her husband said. "To save your life."

Sundays, as soon as the weather warmed, my grandfather headed for the beach: Nantasket, Wellfleet, Revere. He took his youngest daughter with him. Once they took the ferry to Martha's Vineyard, came home in the moonlight, my grandfather "turned to silver," my mother says, "like a sculpture of a famous man."

In sleep, a bride in Pittsburgh, my mother returned to the ocean. Pa swung her over the waves. Their laughter rolled in again from that horizon line where memories bob like daring swimmers, like sailboats out too far for safety, rolled in to break beautifully and ferociously on the clean sand, whose warmth she felt again in the landlocked rooms she lived in now, pieces of cardboard wedged against the cold in gaps between windows and frames. She would wake with the taste of salt in her mouth, her cheeks stiff with salt, her eyes red from its sting. "Nightmares," she lied to my father as he tried to console her. "Such terrible dreams."

They had lived in Pittsburgh for two years, but she was not used to it at all. My grandfather wrote her letters in his graceful hand: *Is it true you pay double for Blue Cross there? Are all the fish in the rivers dead?*

The fish were not dead, but she hated the acrid smell from the mills, the furniture thick with soot, the mill whistles whining like wolves. Raised there, my father knew all the tricks for living in that sullied place, and he tried to teach them to her.

"It hurts to breathe," she would complain.

"Breathe like this, through your nose," he would tell her, a hand over his mouth as he demonstrated.

"The clothes get dirty as soon as I hang them on the line."

"Hang them in the bathtub," he would say, and one

5

night came home with a drying rack for his wife to set in the claw-footed tub.

"In the middle of the day it's dark!" she would cry.

He would turn on all the lights in the apartment. "Now see? Who needs sunshine when you got Edison?"

"The ocean," she would weep. "I miss the beach."

And he would take her for walks around the municipal reservoir, the filtration plant's machinery churning in her ears.

It was 1942. My mother was three months pregnant with me, her ankles already swollen, her small breasts ballooning, the dark mother line descending from her navel like the path of an anchor dropped into the sea. "I don't recognize myself," she said. "I don't know who I am."

"Don't talk foolish," my father said. "You're my wife."

In December, he was drafted. They had known he would be, but my parents were not people for whom the abstract future held much currency. She handed him a letter that had arrived that morning. He read in a quavering voice, as if the news were unexpected: "Greetings."

"I can't stay here alone," she said.

"You can stay with Lena," he said. His aunt and uncle lived two buildings down. "They have the extra room since Sammy joined."

"I'll go home," she said, reminding him of her heart's geography.

They packed up all their personal belongings. As each item disappeared into a container, it seemed to my mother that her young marriage itself was being dismantled, undone: a steamer trunk of clothing, towels, muslin sheets; a carton of chipped dishes, service for four, the Silver Rose pattern she'd found at the thrift shop where she'd also discovered the gilt-framed Rembrandt reproduction, one dollar, that she'd bought my father for his twenty-eighth birthday. A high school teacher had noticed his talent, provided him with sketching pads my father's parents could

6

not afford. For three years, my father spent all his spare time filling the pages with drawings of bridges and birds and horse-drawn ice wagons plodding up slick cobble-stoned hills. When he'd begun to love art more than any-thing else, knowing it would keep him poor forever (he had read that painters starved, turned to absinthe and cocaine, were always being evicted from wretched quarters in the worst sections of Paris and New York), knowing this hobby could turn into an addiction, he threw his pen-cils away and hid the pads in the back of his closet. Years later, I discovered them in a cardboard carton on which he'd printed ART WORK. I praised the fine detail, the subtle composition, the purity of line.

"So what?" he said. "Once upon a time, I had a knack. Now I'm just another working stiff."

Stiff was accurate. In the produce yards, he'd arrive at 4 A.M. to begin unloading the crates of fruits and veg-etables the farmers brought in their pickup trucks, then reloading the goods into the vans of merchants who came to haggle with the farmers over the day's offerings. For my father, the pay was meager but dependable. In the beginning, he dreamed of a produce store someday, "being my own man," tried to see his years in the yards as "train-ing in the business." To his new wife, who had come to Pittsburgh one summer and been pursued by my father from bumper cars to Ferris wheel to merry-go-round in Kennywood Amusement Park, he brought gifts: bagfuls of bruised tomatoes, scarred peppers, lettuce going brown, dented apples, overripe bananas—a bounty salvaged from the trash bin. My mother made stews and soups, apple-sauce, banana bread. She grew proud of her domestic re-sourcefulness, resentful that it was required.

What she wanted from him was one perfect melon, exotically sweet. If only once he had splurged, she might have forgiven him his common sense.

A year after her wedding and departure from Boston,

7

my grandfather sent my mother a present: a lace collar, brand new, from the upper levels of Filene's. Never mind that he had never given his own wife such a fine offering. He had no rival for his wife, no need for a canny courtship that struck the precisely right note between lament and aplomb. What he arrived at was a rather irresistible dignity that was, in fact, his actual nature.

Sometime during those first two years of her marriage, my mother would catch my father staring at Rembrandt's portrait of the aristocrat in the plumed helmet, and my father looked chastened to her, as if rebuked by the elegance of the headpiece, the privileged angle of the head, as if my father suspected that my mother might have bought him this particular print for reasons not entirely testimonial. When my father talked about making ends meet, was he talking less about money than his own cloven self?

She took down the Rembrandt from its place in the room that served as both parlor and bedroom. French doors camouflaged the bed that folded up into the wall, hidden away like dreams and sex. She took down the shirred organdy curtains she'd made from four yards she'd discovered in the remnant box at Woolworth's. In newspaper, she wrapped the photographs she'd kept on the bureau and placed them in a canvas satchel: her parents, two immigrants keeping an eye on their American daughter.

My grandfather was waiting for her at the station. It was snowing. The glittering flakes stuck to his thin white hair, to the shoulders and sleeves of his old tweed overcoat, even to the tops of his age-stained hands. As the train steamed into his view, my mother tells me, he lifted his arms in greeting and the platform lights transformed them into shining wings. She says a crown seemed to shimmer on his head.

I called him "Pa" as my mother did, and he never objected. His was the thumb I grasped from my crib. His was the cheek against whose stubble my own softness was revealed to me. His arm was a raft I floated on inside the bathroom sink where he bathed me.

"He was getting you ready for swimming," my mother says. "To be happy in the water."

His voice speaking my name.

I took my first steps toward him. He was the goal toward which I aspired, the reward of his hug sharpening my instinctive ambition.

When he left the house for the store, I spent the hours of his absence mimicking him. I reinvented his presence by wearing his shoes, my tiny feet lost in the leather boats in which I sailed back and forth across the floor. I stood at the parlor window as he did, watching the street, observing the birds that nested in the maple, my hands clasped behind my back, my forehead pressed to the glass so that my breath, as his, clouded the pane. I chanted some loose imitation of the prayers he intoned when he woke and before he went to sleep, my body swaying like his, my eyes closed to this world. In the kitchen, I pulled newspapers from his stack beside the icebox, spread them on the linoleum, pretended to lose myself as he did in words I could not yet read; still, the print felt alive to me, the letters moved like tiny animals beneath my finger. Later I would come to learn that he was the man from whom I learned transcendence; but in those early years, before I needed words to justify devotion, I simply did what Pa did. I loved him. When he came home at the end of the day, I sat on the seat he made of his ankles, I grasped his hands, I rode the ship his body became, and we shouted together like sea gulls swooping down from the sky to the beach, then up again, up, into the unpeopled heights.

By the time my father came home from the service, I was already my grandfather's child.

The stranger, my father, drove up in a taxi my mother seemed to will into view, that was how deeply she concentrated on the corner around which it turned; then down the block it cruised of onetime Victorian mansions converted now into rental units, dumbwaiters boarded up, closets for fancy wardrobes made over into bathrooms, clotheslines strung across the yards in which wealthy families once lolled, or played croquet, or convalesced.

My mother had dressed me in starched organdy, bought me my first pair of Mary Janes and anklets edged with lace, secured a pink bow in my wispy curls. My mother and grandparents were dressed up as well, in their best clothes, their faces serious, anxious, as if they doubted that my father was truly returning, or feared what his return implied. We waited in the front yard on that cool October afternoon, the sun's light thinned out, bleached, falling almost like a crust of ice on the leafless branches of the sycamores and elms. On that kind of day that is as much the end of something as the beginning, we could have been a rich family of another time, awaiting a hearse or a wedding coach, grieving or celebrating, it would be hard to decipher which.

The stranger, my father, climbed out of the cab.

He wore his Navy whites and looked like the uniformed man in the photograph on my mother's dresser. She had taken me to the picture every evening before bed, as other children are led through prayers, or read to, or taught little rhymes with which they can console themselves in the dark.

"This is your daddy," she would say, and take my hand and lay it against the glass.

Was I supposed to feel my father's face coming to life against my palm? I did not understand her ritual. I had not known what was expected of me, nor did I now.

"That's your daddy," my mother said.

Her voice broke. She ran down the front walk and embraced the stranger. He kissed her on the mouth. Daddy? I held onto Pa's leg, my face pressed against the familiar gabardine; his hand cupped my head, a proprietary gesture.

My father kissed my grandmother, shook Pa's hand, then hugged him with one arm. The other arm cradled a box bound by a thick red ribbon and an oversized bow; he'd left his duffel bag at the curb. Even as he greeted my grandfather, my father's eyes fixed on me. Tears clustered in his lashes and his gaze seemed to require of me a reciprocal intensity. Now he knelt down to my level. He held out the present to me. He said my name. He knew me. Later I would learn that he had kept my picture taped to the bottom of the bunk above his, so that when he went to sleep at night and when he woke in the morning, the first thing he saw was not a Betty Grable pinup, or even a photograph of his wife, but me, an infant on a blanket spread out on the grass in Franklin Park.

I said nothing. He was a stranger. I did not know him. I turned my face back into the fabric of my grandfather's trouser leg, and he allowed me the refuge.

"Give your daddy a kiss," my mother instructed, but Pa kept his hand on my head, his claim to me clear.

Against such odds my father rose. He took my mother's hand. They mounted the porch steps, his gift to me still unaccepted, the transaction unaccomplished.

Pa and I followed.

My grandmother trailed us all, sighing. Perhaps one of her many ailments—she would be dead by winter—had flared up, or this homecoming had disappointed her, or she was sad because in a few hours it would be time to take off her good dress and who could say when another occasion for wearing it might arise.

Nana died in January, three months after my father's return. My mother tells me her parents' marriage "wasn't good." She tells me anecdotes that support that interpretation. By the time I was born, Nana was a woman who stayed in bed, rising only to complain about something for which no remedy existed: the war, the weather, the passing of time. She was too absorbed with her ailments, her deprivations, her husband's lack of drive to offer her daughter or grandchild much notice. "Did I come to America to lose everything I had?" Nor did our presence bring her solace. She was inconsolable, which I have come to learn is a clinical term, a disease, and perhaps it was chronic unhappiness that killed her, that rendered her less than alive to me even before she died. My sense of her remains abstract and vague, as much of my memories of Pa are concrete, sensuous, embodied. But did they have feelings for each other that my mother failed to recognize? In spite of the bickering, the criticism, the silences, the averted eyes, did they love each other?

For weeks after her death in the hospital, where she'd faded away like a dimming lightbulb or a radio signal growing weaker until at last it leaves the range of human reach, Pa walked the rooms of our flat, not so much searching for his wife as assuring himself of her disappearance. A dozen times a day he spoke her name; silence answered; he nodded. He held her shawl in his arms, the one she'd wrapped around her bulk regardless of the season or the temperature in the house, and the near weightlessness of the garment testified: she is gone. He sat on her side of their bed and studied the emptiness, the sheer negation suggested by the space where she had lain. One day I found him there, the fingers of one hand stroking the opened palm of the other.

"This is Lithuania," he said, stroking the map of his own flesh. "Your nana came from . . . right there."

He stared at the spot until it transformed itself into a peopled town; I saw him watching a world I could not see. Even after he went back to his store, resumed his life, took up again his newspapers, his gardening, his grandchild—still some part of him remained where I found him that day, with the young girl he had married from a town that no longer existed on any map—the Nazis had leveled the place, obliterated it—save the one in his mind.

My mother's grieving took a different form: a series of illnesses that seemed like a speeded-up version of Nana's life. In a single month, my mother contracted bronchitis, middle-ear infection, "stomach trouble," water on the knee. It was left to my father, at the time without a job, to care for me.

He took me to the park and I would not play: I froze at the top of the slide until he let me climb backward down the ladder; I dug my toes into the ground to stop the swing he pushed; I let the ball he threw me sail beyond me into the prickly bushes. He cooked meals I left on my plate. He filled the tub for my bath and I drained it. Finally, he withdrew from the effort, and I blamed him for this too, though I knew I would resist all his appeals, all his suggestions. I knew what he refused to admit: Nana had died to make room for him. I was losing everyone, in one way or another. Pa divided now between past and present, my mother always ill, Nana dead. I had even been evicted from the room I shared with my mother. When my father returned, I was moved to a corner of the parlor. A junior bed, a maple chest, a floor lamp, a small trunk that held my toys: these were the furnishings in the area that came to be considered my "room" as surely as if walls had risen around it, a door hinged to an invisible frame.

I was learning the ways in which adults could impose on children realities for which no evidence existed: "This is your father, this is your room, there is no reason in the world for you to be so unhappy." In the room my parents now occupied, the door closed "for privacy," I listened easily to every word of their arguments.

"It's time to make plans to go home," he said.

"He won't come," she said, referring to Pa, meaning herself.

"Then he'll live with your sister." Aunt Joan and her family had a bungalow in Revere, four blocks from the ocean.

"He can't get to his store from Revere," she said. "He'll be lost."

"I'm lost here."

He drove a milk truck for a few months; he worked as a letter sorter for the post office; he sold Uncle Herb's Vitamin Tonic door-to-door.

"In the yards," he said, "I'm established. In Pittsburgh, I know my way around. I know the people."

After Nana died, she had said, "Pa needs you, he needs an assistant."

"He needs me like a hole in the head. There aren't enough customers for him to wait on himself."

"He means for you to have it after him."

"I don't want it. When will you hear what I'm telling you?"

I heard.

My mother told me, "We have to break up the house."

I was five years old. When she first used those words weeks before to describe this day that had now arrived with no greater signal than the low whine of the moving van that had taken its place outside, when my mother had said, "We have to break up the house," I had imagined terrible destruction. Windows would shatter, floors would buckle and splinter, ceilings and walls would cave in on themselves. Nights, forcing myself to prepare for the day of terror, I could nearly smell the crumbling plaster, almost feel the night air whip through the shell of the dying house.

My mother had worked out all the details of the plan. The furniture would be sold to our landlord, Mr. Pinsky, who would disperse the pieces to furnished flats he rented out all over the city. My grandfather's store would be liquidated and he would go to live with Aunt Joan. My mother

14

and I would leave Boston on the night train to join my father in Pittsburgh, where he had been waiting for months for us to "make the move already."

As she made these decisions, finally, after months of tortured refusals and procrastinations, I imagine my mother was stunned by how simply, how logically, how inevitably the plan took form: as if each decision were a spoke on a wheel to which she had been bound without knowing it, on whose momentum she would travel the rest of her life, as surely as the night train would bear her and her child into the darkness.

I had gone with Pa to the store on his last day. I loved to visit there, dressing up in shabby costumes, listening to my grandfather converse in Yiddish with neighbors who came looking for a good winter jacket, a serviceable pair of woolen trousers. Now the old coats and suits and battered hats were gone from the racks and shelves. I helped him soap the windows. He swept the floor, pushing the broom heavily across the worn oak planks. Our voices sounded hollow, lost in the emptiness. We collected the last pieces of litter in a cardboard carton, and together we dragged the box to the curb. He padlocked the door, and on the tarnished doorknob we hung the FOR RENT sign with which the landlord had entrusted him. He took my hand. Without looking back a single time, we walked home.

"You're sixty-seven years old," my mother told him that evening. "You deserve a retirement."

"Like Jonah deserved a whale."

"You won't make this a little bit easy for me?"

"You want I should show you how I really feel? You want I should jump off the roof right now?"

While the workers moved, I sat on a crate and watched them carry out piece after piece of the household I loved. They worked slowly, grunting under their burdens. It was July, hot, the air dead with heat. The movers' faces gleamed

15

with sweat, and soon they took off their shirts and their brown-skinned bodies looked like a piano's polished wood, each man like a carved African idol, an ebony warrior. I had seen pictures of them in *National Geographic*, tribal icons discovered in the tombs of long-buried chieftains. Perhaps my grandparents' lamps and chairs and dressers and beds were offerings of some sort, perhaps the huge van that rested out front like a giant coffin on wheels was a repository for treasures promised a thousand years ago to an undying spirit. That was no more strange than my mother's explanation: "Just because people love each other doesn't mean they stay together." Why not? I asked. "The world has its reasons," my mother said, as if the planet itself had a brain and a heart. She shook her head mournfully. "Don't think I understand it better than you do. I don't."

Pa did not jump off a roof. His suicide was subtle, carried out in stages over the course of a year, kindly in that it allowed for other interpretations: hardening of the arteries, senility, geriatric diseases for which no names had yet been invented but that surely could account for his decline.

"He was old," my mother tells me. "You wouldn't realize. For you, he always had energy. But he was an old man."

First he stopped talking. Aunt Joan called from Revere: "I can't get him to say a word," she told my mother. "You try."

My mother coaxed and demanded. She pleaded. In the apartment we lived in now, the flowers and yards of my life in Boston abandoned for bricks and alleys and hallways thick with strangers, I was emptying the dollhouse my father had bought me of all its fragile furniture. I stashed the pieces under the bed. I undressed the family of tiny dolls who were meant to live in the once-intact household and assigned each member, alone and naked, to a different barren room. My mother called me from the kitchen. I came to the doorway.

"It's Pa," she said, as if I hadn't listened to her entire half of the conversation. "He wants to talk to you."

But I knew that could not be true. I had heard her say, "This is a crazy thing you're doing, Pa, refusing to speak."

Well, crazy or not, he had chosen it. He had not chosen anything else that had happened to him the last year. I would not take the phone. I would not violate his freedom. I would not tempt him out of his dignity. Behind my burning eyes, my locked lips, my breath stilled like an ocean in which the tide suddenly ceases to operate, I joined him in his silence. I joined him.

"Talk to him," she said.

I went to my room. I got into bed. I was six years old, and I would never see my grandfather again. For five days, I kept mute like Pa, we protested together, and no entreaty on my parents' part was strong enough to sunder that connection, no wooing or threat capable of interrupting that long, long conversation.

2

On the same day that Czar Alexander II was blown to bits a few miles from the Winter Palace in St. Petersburg, my great-grandmother screamed, "I'm dying! I'm dying!" in the back room of her wooden house in the town of Volkovysk, and my grandfather was born into history.

This was March, 1881.

This was his birthright: bombs, blood, shattered glass.

History would not intend for him to be gentle. He would not intend to argue with History, but he was a man of character and had no choice.

Character, we are told, begins in the womb. The struggle to be one's self begins in that dark jostling carriage, a nine-month ride that ends in an explosion not unlike the blast that brought Alexander's coach crashing to the cobblestones, the felled horses bleating like terrified babies. In his mother's womb, my grandfather was already a child of turmoil, already learning to withstand the convulsions of the world.

His mother. I have one picture of her, the paper so riddled with cracks that her young face looks prematurely aged, as if an entire life has been compressed into a single image. Say her name was Simca. Say she was a professional mourner, a woman paid to wail at funerals, paid to sit on the hill above the graves of the dead and sing to the ghosts. The dead required reassurance. Having relinquished their bodies, the dead listened for the living, who chanted, *You are still among us, you are still here.* To Simca, the dead sang to her in return, though others less attuned to their voices could have mistaken those responses for wind, or crows, or the gravedigger's shovel ringing against the rocky earth.

How did she come to such a vocation?

When did my great-grandmother first acknowledge her talent for sorrow, first discover the immense range of her grief?

In this legend I am inventing, she is five years old, sweeping out the shed where her father keeps his hoes and rakes. He is in the yard, scattering seed to the chickens.

18

"Look, Simca!" he calls to her as they work. "Look at the moon!"

The moon in the morning? What should a child make of such an aberration? She comes to the door to witness the sky's confusion. Has God forgotten the order of things, is he changing the rules of the universe? There are miracles, she has heard her father say, and curses. Which is this, this collapse of distinction between night and day? The chickens are running in circles, colliding into each other. Are they, too, befuddled by the sight of the moon in the morning sky?

No.

Two drunken peasants have wandered into the yard, their mud-caked boots stirring up dust and seed. One of the men kicks at each chicken into which he blunders, yells curses at them, and the injured creatures flap their helpless wings. Simca climbs up on a barrel to stare through the cobwebbed window. The strangers push her father to the ground, his voice flies out of his mouth to heaven—*Aiii! Aiii!*—and Simca sends up her own cry, only to find it lodged like a nail at the base of her throat. When at last the strangers stumble from the yard, her father looks less like a man than a huge slaughtered chicken on the blood-drenched ground.

For three days Simca did not utter a word, and it was feared she would never speak again. But on the fourth day she began a week of faint moans, much like the cries of a newborn kitten, and then the moans grew in intensity and volume until finally, two weeks after her father's murder, Simca was screaming the way she had tried to scream in the shed. It was less a cry of terror than a cry of loss. It incorporated into its timbre the acceptance of death. It contained no plea of help, or any conviction that help was possible. It was the mourner's cry, and it caused Simca's mother, exhausted by her own bereavement, to say "She has lost her childhood now"; and believing her daughter now knew all the world had to teach about suffering, believing there was no more comfort she could offer, she rose at last from her vigil by the side of Simca's bed and began once again the rituals of her now-husbandless household.

Thus abandoned, Simca developed a stoop, a slow gait, became known as "the girl with the long face," and began turning up in the village at funerals of people she barely knew. It was her apprenticeship. As the rabbi intoned the *Kaddish* and rocked to a rhythm Simca came to understand was the continual shuddering of the dead in their graves, as the relations wept with what Simca came to learn was their small allotment of tears from God's endless supply, as she heard over and over again the first clod of earth heaved against each coffin's lid until she realized that the thud was part of an endless ceremonial beating upon the scarred drum of eternity—as all these things became clear to Simca in ways for which she had no words, she opened herself to her calling as an artist assents to the colors burning behind her eyes or the music rising through the long columns of her bones or the poems reading themselves aloud in the silent realm of her heart.

It was at the cemetery that she met the man she would marry.

Of Isaac Lieb there is also one picture, but so yellowed he is a blur. Nothing remains but the fact of his bulk and the aristocratic posture with which he faced the camera's smoky discharge. At fifteen, he had become a tailor's assistant, replacing the tailor's own son, who had left Volkovysk for Lodz, where he was involved in what the tailor referred to as "activities." Inside the son's abandoned workbench, Isaac discovered a cache of Socialist pamphlets, a dog-eared *Das Kapital* in Yiddish translation, protest poems copied on scraps of paper: a rebel's library.

Isaac's political education.

He read late at night, after he finished with the daily

buttonholes, the hems, the mending, the occasional alteration, the infrequent construction of a new garment for one of the local merchants who brought a piece of wool or a length of cotton cloth or a few yards of linen sent by a wealthy relative in Vilnius or Kiev. Laboring one night over such a project—a linen smock to be embroidered around the neckline and sleeves with rosettes and worn at her daughter's wedding by the shoemaker's wife—Isaac Lieb saw in the rippling white fabric the milk for which hungry babies cried and saw in the rosettes he had woven with fine scarlet thread the blood of Jews and peasants pitted against each other by the Czar's soldiers, and seeing the wedding smock transformed in his very hands into a tapestry of injustice, Isaac raised his scissors in the air and let out the screams of a man in battle, brought down the blades in great slashes through the newly finished blouse until there was nothing left of it but a mound of ragged strips piled by his feet on the scrap-littered floor.

"Cossacks!" he said, when the tailor cried out for the perpetrator of the garment's destruction. "If I hadn't run them off, everything in the shop would have been ruined!"

The tailor gave Isaac a raise, and as Isaac accepted the reward for his lie, he appeared humble and grateful. But inside himself, his arm hoisted the scissors again and again. At seventeen, Isaac had become a revolutionary.

In the spring, his mother died of influenza—he himself had been sick for weeks with a lesser bout; his chest ached from coughing; when he walked he hugged his ribs as if he had just been beaten—and the family buried her in the rain.

Simca had spread a burlap tarp on her place on the hill and covered herself with another that she had dipped at home in paraffin, which had dried to a waterproof sheen. Thus protected, she sat at her mourning post and watched the Lieb family slosh through the mud to the gravesite. The father and three sons bore the coffin. One of the brothers had to stop every few steps to clear his congested lungs. As they moved closer to her, Simca could hear the others pleading with the sick one to drop his share of the burden, and she could see his hand grip his mother's bier even more resolutely, his shoulder on which the pine box rested seeming to form new muscles as he walked.

His eyes, she thought, seeing how they fixed on a place beyond any landmark; they are looking for death.

And when her trembling abated, she thought, As are mine.

For the first time since her father's murder, Simca felt stirrings of kinship, a fluttering in her belly not unlike the first movements of a child in the womb.

Brother, she named Isaac Lieb before she had spoken a word to him. Husband.

This is their wedding night: it is winter in Volkovysk, and a veil of snow covers each rickety house and shed and shop, each market stall, each gravestone in the cemetery, each hitching post, garden plot, and stone well, the main pump, the dirt roads that wind now like silk ribbons through the town. Volkovysk looks less like a town than a memory of a town, or a dream of a town not yet created. Looking out the window as Isaac sits on the edge of the bed—they will live in her mother's house, this will be their room, the mother is spending the night at a neighbor's—hearing him undo the laces of his boots, Simca thinks, This is not real, I am not here, this is not my life. Either because she is too happy or too afraid or probably both, she grips the shutters when he comes to stand behind her, wills herself through the glass and across the frigid earth to the stone slab under which her father lies in his unrelenting silence—he is the one ghost who refuses to answer her song of lament with his own—wills herself there and kneels in the virgin snow and remains there all night, safe in her familiar isolation, glad to be cold and separate again.

Even though Isaac believes she is with him in the bed

on which their bodies fuse, she thinks triumphantly, I am not here! Afterward, when Isaac wipes her wet cheeks with his palm, Simca is shocked to find that she has been weeping, for she does not weep in the cemetery; she wails but she does not weep. Weeping belongs to a life which is not hers anymore, which died with her childhood that day in the shed, and she kisses his salty hand over and over again to taste, for the first time since her father's murder, her own tears, sour and warm.

Wife, thinks Isaac, savoring what he believes to be her passion for him. You are my wife.

Months passed. In spite of the gift of tears, Simca remained unable to follow her body into the realm of pleasure. Her mouth would cry out, her limbs would grow supple as the reeds which swayed at the river's edge, and in the place where Isaac had entered her, she would feel herself change into water, feel the waves grow wild and high, then ebb, becalmed to the depths. Yet even then, some crucial piece of herself remained, as on that first night, chaste, unmoved, wed only to that early grief.

Although Isaac did not complain about his wife's ultimate estrangement, she was sure he sensed it. She consulted the rabbi's wife, who recommended herb tonics and promised special prayers. In the cemetery, Simca confided in those spirits whose earthly lives had been particularly lusty, but they had already forgotten their flesh and could give her no advice.

After a year, she grew fearful that Isaac had taken a mistress. Surely he was yearning for someone who did not stand partly outside their bedroom like a boarder pacing the kitchen after the family members have all gone to sleep. Where did he really go two and three nights a week after putting in twelve-hour days in the tailor's shop? Political meetings, he told her. Secret discussions. She believed him less and less, and finally one evening she followed him through the darkened town to what she was sure was a rendezvous with the glazier's widow.

Simca followed him as quietly as the ghost she believed herself to be, three quarters of a mile to Lev Kolsky's blacksmith shop. In the doorway, Lev greeted Isaac with a kiss on each cheek and ushered him into the dim store, one small oil lamp burning under Lev's worktable. She hid herself in the bushes beneath the window and watched. Eight men sat on the floor in a circle, and their shadowy forms melded together so that Simca could not tell where one man began and the other ended, so that only the circle itself had definable substance, and each man's voice was only as real as the voice to which it responded or to which it directed a question. Words broke free of sentences and flew past her ear: oppression, exploitation, proletariat, ideology. The men spoke the foreign terms with fluency and zeal. They understood each other as Simca and her ghosts understood each other. They were—oh, she saw it clearly in the way their eyes glittered more brightly than the lantern could possibly account for!—enraptured.

She had been wrong, and right. There was no other woman. But in Lev Kolsky's night-shrouded shop, she had witnessed her husband's clandestine romance. He was in love with History. He possessed it as he would a mistress, with the blind, erotic dedication of a lover.

She turned her eyes from the window. He will be killed the way my father was killed.

She walked home. Her mother was already asleep. Simca put on her best muslin gown and waited for Isaac in their bed. Hours later, when he returned from the meeting of the Volkovysk Bund, she whispered to her husband, "I am here, Isaac"—meaning, Now this is real, this is my life—and my grandfather, Nathan Lieb, was conceived.

Simca's mother was elated that her daughter was pregnant. The old woman had long feared that her daughter was less alive than other people in the town. Sometimes the old woman would question Ilka Blum, the proprietress of the mikva.

"Does she look . . . healthy? I mean, does everything seem the way it should in a bride, I mean normal?"

Ilka, who had worked at the ritual bathhouse behind the synagogue for thirty-two years, assured the old woman over and over that Simca was "nice and clean and nothing growing and nothing shriveled up. Believe me, soon the house will be full of grandchildren, she won't have time anymore for funerals and graves."

No time for funerals and graves? The old woman reminded Ilka that she could no longer bake the fifty loaves of challah each week whose sale for the Sabbath had long supported her and Simca. The old woman's fingers were crippled with arthritis; each finger had become a rigid hook like the ones on which the town butcher had hung the chickens Simca's father used to raise. If Simca gave up her mourning work for motherhood, the old woman worried, Isaac's salary would not be sufficient for the three of them. Ilka Blum lowered her head to her great bosom, rubbed her breasts as a gypsy might caress her crystal ball.

"Let the girl take in laundry then," she counseled.

One night the old woman dreamed of Simca hauling bushel after bushel of wet laundry to the cemetery, draping each gravestone with the shirts and dresses and trousers and nightgowns, even with the underwear, of the residents of Volkovysk. Around the perimeter of the cemetery, the naked townspeople cried out for their clothes, but Simca admonished them—"The dead are cold, they need your garments more than you do!"—and continued to wend her way through the maze of burial markers she knew with the authority of a longtime citizen, distributing apparel to the invisible populace with whom she so easily conversed.

Many mornings now Simca had to stay in bed, sipping

hot water and lemon, nibbling on a piece of dry bread, waiting for the noon hour when the nausea ceased. As if her body were now in league with the earth's rotation around the sun. As if her body, after years of being adrift in numbness, were now connected to the rhythms of the living, sensate world. She felt disloyal withdrawing so much energy from sorrow. The disembodied were her compatriots as surely as the members of the Bund were Isaac's, yet here she was attending to her physical self with a seriousness that bordered on obsession. It was not simply that her abdomen was changing from its familiar flat plane into an expanding globe, the weight of which pressed down on her bladder and shot flashing pain down her thighs and tugged at the small of her back. Her skin darkened, and she studied her face daily in the mirror, marking the advance of altered pigmentation. Her ankles and fingers swelled, and she soaked them in tubs of hot water. She broke out into sweats on the coolest of days. Sometimes she was so hungry that she wanted to grab the food from the plates of Isaac and her mother and eat all their portions herself; sometimes the smell of cooked meat drove her from the table to vomit up the last meal she had eaten. Her breasts doubled in size, and her inverted pale nipples turned full and brown. Sometimes a small misfortune— the end of a somber dream, or the sight of a delicate insect entrapped in a spider's web, or a piece of crockery slipping accidentally from her wet hands—triggered in Simca depths of sadness that not even years among graves had been able to touch. She would sob for hours; it seemed as if the very world had shattered at her feet.

But more often, Isaac would tell a joke or a neighbor's child would make a funny face or the cat would brush by and tickle her leg, and Simca would embark on a fit of laughter so prolonged it was as if she had entered a state in which all the joy she had denied herself since childhood had accumulated in a secret pouch beneath her heart and was now releasing itself in a great rush of happiness throughout her body. On the days she was able to get to the cemetery, she felt a double sense of betrayal: first, to the spirits, whose language she seemed to be forgetting; and second, to the baby inside her, who seemed to grow as still as death when Simca came to mourn. When Isaac returned home on those days, she would have him put his ear to her belly to listen for the baby's heart, and she began to realize, toward the end of her term, that she would spend the rest of her earthly existence torn between the demands of the living and the needs of the dead, with no sense of where her true allegiance lay, exhausted by her confusion, more alone than ever.

Grandfather, you were three months old when Isaac announced, "We are moving to Vilnius."

Simca was nursing you when Isaac delivered what was for her a decree of banishment, and suddenly your tiny head began to root around as if in search of a third breast: the moment that Isaac had spoken, Simca's milk dried up. She swore that she actually felt the ducts around her nipples close, actually witnessed her laden breasts diminish in size by half. You howled for days. The scalded milk she fed you with a spoon did not appease your deeper hunger for the body to which you were still attached in your imagination, and you would push your tongue against the metal bowl in an effort to expel what was for you an alien substance, an absolutely inadequate substitution for the soft familiar flesh you craved, whose texture and smell you still retained in that constant dream that is our infancy.

Simca spent hours by the stove in the kitchen, applying hot compresses to her atrophied breasts, but she knew the treatments were irrelevant. The dead residents of Volkovysk who depended on Simca for news and encouragement and the kind of attention that made invisibility bearable had heard Isaac's announcement. Taking her milk, she knew, was just the first of their tactics for keeping her with them. Nights, she could hardly sleep, waiting for blindness, or paralysis, or the sudden loss of all her auburn hair, which Isaac, in defiance of Jewish tradition, had implored her not to cut. It did not matter to the dead that Simca wanted to stay. They were beyond the consolations of intent. They existed solely in the less-subtle dimension of action, and Simca's protestations that leaving Volkovysk was not her idea or desire failed to move their buried hearts. They felt abandoned, and they were striking out at her in the first throes of their grief, as the living often curse the corpse of one they have needed and loved.

Isaac Lieb could not understand his wife's hysteria. She had never been happy in Volkovysk. She did not socialize with the other women at the well or at the market, and she did not chat with them in the women's section of the synagogue or join in the gossip they traded in whispers even as the rabbi read aloud from the Torah. As for her work as a mourner, didn't she come home silent and despondent, didn't it take her a good hour to recover from the morbid occupation into which she had stumbled for want of better opportunities in such a provincial town?

When Simca tried to speak to Isaac about her conversations with the dead, he would tell her, "The revolution does not have time for phantoms, Simca."

And he would begin his lectures, which sometimes lasted half the night, about the socialism of Marx and Bakunin and Tkachev and a society where being a Jew did not result in a little girl watching her father being hacked to death.

Simca would listen with the concentration of a child who may be fixed on the adult's words, or possibly enthralled during the oration with the speaker's eye movements, or a birthmark shaped like a butterfly, or the way in which the adult's jaw hinges and unhinges with each syllable. But whether she actually learned anything from Isaac is debatable; it was Isaac who commanded her attention. His presence, the facts of his body and voice. Brother. Husband. Of his mistress, Politics, she wanted to know as little as possible, but she never told him that, so he continued to try to bring them together, mistress and wife in intimate relation, and Simca continued her silent resistance to such a ménage.

What he had not told her was that he had decided to move to Vilnius ever since that day three months earlier, the day of your birth, Grandfather, when the group of urban radicals who called themselves "The People's Will" had finally succeeded in assassinating Alexander II. Holding his newborn infant in his arms, Isaac vowed to you to break free of the shtetl—the wooden house, the cemetery, the tailor's bench, Lev Kolsky's blacksmith shop—to leave Volkovysk for good, where time seemed to lie as still as a stagnant pool, to bring his child into the city, into the rushing waters of ideas and events, into the revolution, into what Isaac Lieb truly believed would be the great and glorious liberation of History.

3

It is true: all I have of Simca and Isaac are the photographic distortions my mother found in the top bureau drawer in my grandfather's room, Jewish Home for the Aged and Infirm, January 1950. Not even anecdotes fed to me in my childhood. On the subject of his parents, my grandfather was silent. But I have come to learn that every word we utter pronounces the names of our mothers and fathers, and they speak through our mouths, their voices ride on our breath like boats skimming the river's skin.

Grandfather, I remember the parents you sheltered in your bones. Simca slept in your right eye, Isaac in your left. When I would put my ear to yours as if it were a seashell in which I might have heard the ocean's depths, I heard your father and your mother whispering to each other. And when we walked together in the park, Pa, you supported the weight of your parents, making their journey across your shoulder's span: all your life they traveled on your back.

You were still an infant when they arranged for the trip to Vilnius: two days in a crowded, airless train. The day before the planned departure, Simca took you on a shorter pilgrimage. That morning she bathed you with particular care, and in the metal washtub you relaxed for the first time in the tepid water. One of her hands under your head, the other searched each crevice of your baby's fullness for specks of grime, lint, excretion, encrusted milk. She cleansed each ear as if it were a carving she was polishing, and when she drew you out of the tub and dried your flushed skin, you were a prince curried for court, a groom about to marry; perhaps—I say this gently, Grandfather, but without apology—a corpse prepared for the formal descent into the earth's folds.

It had rained, I imagine, during the night and now the August sun was burning the moisture off the trees and grass and off the cobblestones and tin roofs, the vapor hissing like a secret the morning was telling to anyone who knew how to listen.

You knew how to listen.

With your infant's wisdom, you turned your full attention to the morning's iterations, your head lifting off your mother's shoulder to hear better the messages sailing on the air. *Ssssss. Ssssss. Ssssss.* All the way to the cemetery you concentrated on the sound of water returning to the

30

sky, climbing up the invisible cords that link forever heaven and earth. *Life,* the vapor whispered. *Life. Life.*

Simca, of course, heard other voices. Now that she believed Isaac was resolved to leave Volkovysk for good, now that the crates were packed and the trunk full and the garden plucked of its harvest and given to neighbors they would leave behind and for whom Simca felt sudden stabs of devotion, although she had never had much to do with them, now that she knew her final good-bye to the spirits was inevitable, she regained completely her fluency in their tongue, and she no longer had to be in the cemetery to hear them speak, she heard them even in her sleep; they surrounded her with their ceaseless dirge. Sometimes, Grandfather, you would cry for an hour before Simca even noticed. Sometimes Isaac would talk to her for fifteen minutes before he realized that she had not heard a word. Who could compete with the swelled chorus of the dead?

Now, while she carried you from tomb to tomb, resting longest at the headstone of her father, whose death cries still ruptured her dreams, Isaac's own last curses exploded like musket fire inside his pillaged shop. The soldiers dragged him to the well. Two others carried Lev Kolsky, his unconscious body sagging between them like a sack of grain. From a tree in view of the rabbi's smoldering house, twin nooses swung in the blackened air. A huddle of neighbors, forced to the site, wept. Volkovysk collapsed around them, all splinter and ash. The glazier wailed the *Kaddish,* each ancient syllable a broken-winged bird struggling toward the sky.

"Do the collaborators have anything to say for themselves?"

In the blur of smoke and pain, Isaac could not make out the face of the man who had spoken to him. No matter. The uniform's buttons were burning coals, the sword a lick of white flame. "Long live the revolution!" Isaac screamed, the words ripping like fire through his scorched throat.

And then the bench on which his bound feet rested was kicked away.

And all that remained of the future was one last intake of breath.

And Isaac Lieb entered forever the perfect democracy of the dead.

When Simca saw the smoke drifting up the hill, when she heard her father's *Aiii! Aiii! Aiii!* rising to the cemetery in an endless echo of her childhood nightmare, she jumped with you, Grandfather, into a newly dug grave, covered you both with earth she clawed away from the grave's sides, and when you opened your mouth to howl, she filled it with her breast, which, quite suddenly, was once again engorged with milk. For an hour, Simca nursed you in the grave she feared the two of you might never leave. With a finger, she made holes in the dirt that concealed you both, little tunnels to air and light. Gradually, the cries from the town diminished, and then it was so quiet Simca could hear the worms burrowing through the earth in which she hid.

You slept against her skin as she struggled to keep herself awake; her finger moved more and more slowly through the warm soil. Would it be so bad, she wondered, to go to sleep forever among the spirits she loved, close again to her father, her baby fused again to her body as if he had never been born at all?

You had not been to the graves with your mother since those days in which the still water in which you floated heaved and eddied and you taught youself to survive in the turbulence by willing your pulse motionless, by instructing the currents of your blood to slow, by rendering your furled body hard as a snail's shell, jointless, impervious to the swirling pool in which she bore you to the burial grounds. Even as the waters of her womb crashed about you, you listened—with her or through her—to the songs of the dead, those dolphin voices traveling to you through the rough sea in which you survived.

Be calm, you wanted to tell your mother before you had words. Did you understand then the gift she offered that she did not know she was providing? Did you think, before you had words, I am without illusion, Mama; I will be born with the knowledge of death; in this roiling darkness, the truth of creation shines like a moon I cannot yet see and, Mama, I hear my infant's whimper rattle in the old man's throat I keep inside this baby's neck, I feel my flesh thin to dust beneath this mask of baby's dimpled fat?

If not, I thank her for you, now, your granddaughter says: Simca, how strong a swimmer he became!

"Simca! Simca Lieb! Simca, do you he-e-e-e-ar me!"

It was Ilka Blum, calling from the graveyard.

I am here, Simca answered, but as on that morning in the shed sixteen years ago, Simca's voice lay entombed within her. I am here! I am here! but she was silent as a corpse. Ilka might have given up, trudged back to the wreckage of the town, had not you awakened that moment from your dark sleep, Grandfather, had not your cry surfaced like a bright fish swimming for its life. Ilka sank her hands into the depths from which you called. Her hands clasping your head, Simca using all her strength to push you up, you rose through the narrow channel, a child of History born a second time into the shining ruins of the world.

Ilka carried you down the path to the sacked village, her other arm around the dazed Simca. Townsmen were already ascending the hillside to the cemetery, shovels slung over their shoulders, prayers on their lips. In front of the synagogue, the bodies were assembled, sleeping that sleep

33

for which all other sleep is preparation. Around them the relatives gathered. While Ilka held you, Simca searched for Isaac, and when she recognized his shoes sticking out of the tablecloth with which someone had covered him, her heart split open like a goosedown pillow, she fell upon her husband, she joined him in the silence from which she could not rouse him with her screams.

I want them to be buried together.

I am a bird perched on the granite slab marking the adjoining graves that never existed in the Volkovysk cemetery bulldozed by the Nazis over forty years ago. On that land there is a playground now, perhaps an apartment building, maybe a small plant that manufactures something as innocent as shoes. Archaeologists pass over the site without remark.

No matter.

I keep singing, Pa. I keep singing.

Then I will sing Simca's survival.

I am not ready to lose her, my imaginary ancestor, not even to the solace death would have offered her. She did not die in Isaac's unacknowledging arms. As she lay like a rag doll against his body, warmth began to churn in her legs, rise up her torso, bloom through the stem of her neck to flower in the hollows of her earth-stained cheeks. Perhaps it was the sun's heat entering her flesh. Perhaps it was Isaac's last gift to the woman whose face had always reminded him of the moon. Whatever its source, this warmth empowered her like steam to rise from her stupor, to take back her baby from Ilka's arms, to look one last time at the wreckage of the town, up the hill one last time to the graveyard, where her father's ghost, at last, at last, whispered, "Simca, I never blamed you, never, my dearest child," his words floating down to her like seed pods, carrying in them the next season, the future spinning softly through the ash-thick air.

34

4

When he stood on his toes to look out the window, my grandfather saw churches, the spires and domes of Vilnius' ancient cathedrals rising above the Jewish quarter like a second world. His real father lived there, Isaac, a soul sailing through the weave of crosses as living men rowed along the Neris River on warm afternoons.

In the street-level jewelry shop beneath their flat, Nathan's stepfather fixed watches. Maier Nelkin was bald, stocky, his body a compact and efficient machine. In the morning, after his prayers, he did fifty push-ups, fifty sit-ups, and drank two glasses of water, into which he stirred the juice of a bunch of parsley and a small lemon. This concoction cleaned out his system, he said, emptied him of all evidence that he needed to eat like other men. Over his right eye, he wedged a magnifying glass between the bones of his brow and his cheek, the lens fitting into that socket so securely it seemed as if the eye itself had changed form, altered into this mechanical protuberance. Thus equipped, he descended the stairs to his work. He loved his work. He loved the perfect meshing of the tiny gears. He loved the undeviating regularity of the tick. He loved the clarity of numbers, their inviolate and absolute progression on the watch face. He loved the rigid formality of the hands. He saw in timepieces an example for human conduct. He himself was a model of exactitude, control, routine's triumph over impulse.

What was he doing with a stepson who gazed at the sky while his soup got cold? Who liked to close his eyes and walk the apartment like a blind child, stumbling into furniture, banging into walls? Who woke up in the middle of some nights singing, his small voice a parody of some grander singer in his dreams, Maier Nelkin's sleep ruined?

"He's just a child," Simca said, until the day Nathan followed the ice wagon nearly a mile because, he said, he wondered where it was going, and ended up lost for hours, Simca stuffing her shawl in her mouth like a madwoman muffling her own screams, and Maier having to shut down the shop early and search the winding cobblestoned streets for her errant boy.

"You went too far!" she cried to him, not meaning distance.

My grandfather was six years old now, beyond the confinements of literal interpretation, and so he understood his mother's injunction, that it was meant to govern his curiosity, that it was a sanction on his spirit. Of course he could not submit; of course she knew that. As if in contrition, he laid his head on her lap and wept; as if in forgiveness for this aberrant transgression, she stroked his hair. But what grieved them both was the knowledge that he had ceased to be her solace, that he was no longer Simca's baby, that he would live in this world increasingly apart from her, and that, the world being what it was, she would worry about him for the rest of her life and thereafter. She saw them in a row, her father and her first husband and now her son: her father murdered for his faith, her husband for his Bolshevism, and Nathan heir to their martyrdoms, History waiting for her gentle boy like a kidnapper hidden in the bushes.

She had another baby, a girl, Ruth, not yet two. Simca cared for Ruth with all the devotion that survived the facts that she was Maier Nelkin's child, not Isaac's, that she had been born a week after Simca's mother's death, and Simca, weak from yet another loss, had sickened with pneumonia, the baby taken to Maier's sister for three weeks, Simca's memory of the birth blotted out by fever, so that when Ruth was returned to the household, it was as if a foundling had been deposited at the door, another woman's infant, not Simca's daughter at all.

36

In Simca's tentative hold, Ruth readied herself for spills. An infant devoted to restraint, she perfected unobtrusiveness, immobility, hush. Her appetite dwindled. Her naps lengthened. Her smiles seldom opened into laughter, and she learned to squelch her lusty cry, whimpering instead, the rest of her distress imploding inside her like a withheld sneeze. When she learned to walk, she took three steps, four, then sat down, not afraid as much as disinterested. What did she know anymore of exploration? In her father's presence, she froze entirely, and he praised her stillness. Perhaps she would have remained all her life this mannequin soul if circumstance did not invade Maier Nelkin's household with all the chaos of pogrom, all the upheaval of revolution, all the force of catastrophe or miracle (History decides which, in time).

"Nathan," Simca said, and he had to put his ear to the pillow upon which she lay, her voice was that weak, "Nathan, take care of your sister for me."

Simca said this to my grandfather when he was twelve and she was dying—tuberculosis perhaps, cancer, a stricken heart. She was shrinking in her bed. He could see her bones through the pale membrane her skin had become. Her voice had thinned to a thread of sound, spun out from her body still lodged in this bed, this house, this life whose events she had never understood. Her eyes, too, gazed on him as if from a distance, the glazed brown spheres a reflection of her true eyes somewhere else.

"I am going to be with your father," she told him, not unhappily, an immigrant announcing her destination, her new address written down for her in the language of relatives already established in the territory to which she will travel.

Imagine Maier Nelkin left to raise two children by himself, two children such as these. Nathan had become a good student, but now the Torah was one more preoccupation, one more reason to drift away from a conversation, forget to do his chores, lose track of the hour and read until two in the morning, barely able to lace his shoes the next day, but pleased with himself, as if Maier's scorn made no impression on him whatsoever, as if the boy had another father with whom he consulted, whose approval buoyed him; my grandfather, afloat in dreaminess, swimming in a sea indifferent to time, oblivious to time's fastidious boundaries.

And Ruth. The girl did not even know how to walk to the butcher's to buy the chicken for the Sabbath, making sure the bird was plump enough, fresh. She burned the bread. When Maier gave her his trousers to mend, she stitched the front part of the leg to the back, and when she snipped the threads with a scissors, she sliced the fabric itself. Maier yanked the pants from her hands. "Didn't your mother teach you anything?" he screamed. His face swelled with fury, the veins across his cheeks like purple scars. "If you don't take care of things in this house, who will?"

"I will," Nathan said.

"A boy does not—"

"I will," my grandfather said, and slid his arm under the bed where Ruth was hiding, her body flattened like a mouse between the bedsprings and floor. When his hand reached her back, he felt her shuddering; she was sobbing without making a sound. He eased his sister toward him. She burrowed into the cove of his chest.

Take care of your sister for me. Although he stood no more than three feet away, Maier Nelkin now seemed like a shadow to Nathan while the shadows on the wall assumed dimension, his mother's presence palpable, her voice unwavering, her last whisper amplified and resonant.

"Yes, I will," he said again, answering Simca this time, not his stepfather, making again the promise he understood now in its full gravity. This man for whom they had been burdens even when Simca was alive would become their bully now that she was dead. Nathan's years of reverie, contemplation, dreams which overlaid his waking life like filigree so that even the dreariest days glinted for him—these years came to their conclusion as the moon passes through its phases, achieves its brightness, and yields itself to the darkness until the universe summons again its luminosity. That night the truth of his condition announced itself to my grandfather. He was called Lieb and his sister was Nelkin, but their real name was Orphan. He said it to himself, silently, over and over, mastering his history.

Several times a year a man named Vardys traveled from Klaipeda on the Baltic coast two hundred miles inland to Vilnius. Vardys was his last name, but that was the only way Maier Nelkin referred to him. "Vardys is bringing the amber next week," or "If that bastard Vardys raises his prices again, how will I pay Peschel to cut the stones and polish them and make the rings and bracelets and the pendants, and if I don't have an inventory when a customer comes in, it will go out all around the town: Maier Nelkin's shelves are empty, don't bother to look in there, better go around the corner to Cohen's, and while you're there you might as well take your watch to him, he's probably as good as Nelkin, why make two stops when you can get away with one?"

Vardys opened a sack and spilled the cache of just-mined stones across Maier's counter. My grandfather raised his eyes from the floor he was sweeping to look at the amber, which clattered like marbles over the wood, and at Vardys, grinning down at the jewels as if he were a magician, a sorcerer, not a merchant come to bargain.

"You like my treasure?" Vardys said. He had turned his smile on Nathan. "Come have a closer look."

Nathan rested his broom against the wall. He had never seen Vardys this clearly before. The man was tall, over six feet, but so hunched over that his full height was not apparent; he looked like a predatory bird, his black hair and blanched blue eyes markings of some sort, his jutting Tartar cheekbones and pointy beardless chin a bill in which he trapped prey, impaling them first on his mangled teeth.

"Your stepfather thinks I'm a greedy Gentile," Vardys said. "Would a greedy man give away a piece of amber to a boy?" He drew Nathan's hand into his own, unfurled my grandfather's fingers, and placed a gold-colored stone in his palm. "You see that beetle inside? He's as old as the world."

Then Vardys cackled at that notion, as if the import he attached to the encapsulated bug was a joke he could not keep from enjoying, a ruse he had to savor, but my grandfather ignored the ridicule. He put the nugget in his pocket, he claimed it for himself, he restored to it the worth Vardys tried to cancel with contempt.

"Don't think you can use the boy to testify to your character, Vardys," Maier Nelkin said, and as he spoke, he seemed to discover in his own words a message he had been overlooking, a strategy, a scheme to serve his own interests. With one hand he motioned Vardys closer; with the other he directed Nathan back to his broom on the other side of the shop. The two men huddled, sudden conspirators, allies. Their whispers brushed like bats above my grandfather's head.

They struck a deal. They compromised. They shook hands in the manner of businessmen. Vardys gave Maier a good price on the amber, and Maier gave Vardys Nathan Lieb, Simca's child, a month's free labor from a fourteen-year-old boy about to learn yet another lesson of his legacy.

When Maier Nelkin explained to Nathan this "opportunity" he had arranged for him—one month in Klaipeda, on the Baltic, working for Vardys alongside the amber miners, free board in Vardys' house—my grandfather said quietly, "Thank you," stripping the bully of the pleasure derived from the exercise of unjust power. Maier probed

40

Nathan for distress he could scorn, fear he could mock, recalcitrance he could strike down. All he encountered was my grandfather's mild gaze, unblinkingly kind, and the strange smile the boy always wore when he stared out the window at some sight beyond Vilnius' steepled horizon. "It is all arranged, you have no choice in the matter," Maier said, inventing for himself resistance which he could over-rule. Why wasn't the boy upset? His composure so un-nerved Maier Nelkin that when he arrived at his table in the rear of the shop and resumed work on the broken pocketwatch he had earlier disassembled, he could barely remember his practiced manipulations, his fingers were clumsy and thick, his judgments unreliable. As if he had taken ill, he locked up early, went upstairs, got into his bed, and slept until morning, my grandfather's face slip-ping like a ghost in and out of his stepfather's feverish dreams.

On the train to Klaipeda, Vardys pared his fingernails with a pocketknife, brushing the slivers from his lap so they arched in the air and landed on my grandfather's sleeve. Through the cotton of his shirt, a hive swelled. The itchy welt became one more element in his discomfort. It was hot outside, the fourth day in a dry spell, and hot on the train, and Vardys' body was like a great heat-retaining dune against which my grandfather was pressed.

"How much longer?" Nathan said.

Vardys leaned down to him so that the man's breath riffled my grandfather's earlock. "Longer? Until it rains? Until you're rich? Until your Messiah comes, is that it? Until what, little Jew-boy, how much longer until what?"

And then Vardys laughed, savoring his own wit, be-lieving the interchange finished by his own oratorical flour-ish, when Nathan interrupted the almost cannibalistic pleasure Vardys took in himself by saying, "Until I go with my sister to America."

41

As if the train had lurched to a sudden stop, Vardys pitched forward in his seat, his expression transformed from the baiter's to the friend's. He reached out to my grandfather a steadying hand, as if Nathan, too, had been jolted, and the man's voice, as he said, "You plan to go to America?" lost entirely its caustic edge.

Nathan had not intended to tell anyone—certainly not Vardys—about his plan. He did not even think of it as a plan, but rather as a reality that had not yet taken place, whose unfolding would proceed in its own manner until, like a bulb that one morning pushes its buried green shoot through the earth's crust, opportunity bloomed. Often he imagined himself in America, he and Ruth sharing a light-filled flat, flower boxes at each window, geraniums, petunias, the bright red spikes of salvia. He envisioned a promenade, spacious and clean, along which they'd stroll in the evenings, stopping by a café for spirits and talk with intelligent friends. He could see himself leaving for work in the morning and returning at dusk, but his vision did not include the nature of his labors, only a sense that his livelihood, whatever it was, made him happy enough and did not tire him, so that when he got home he still had energy for reading. He dreamed of a life neither spartan nor extravagant, materially modest, the streets paved or not, he did not care. Half a world away, this country, America, waited for him like a fable, simple and miraculous, into whose cosmology he would be summoned.

"For a very reasonable fee," Vardys said, "I can make the arrangements for you."

And so it was that my grandfather, the vassal of this Vardys, was transformed into the man's next client, the amber merchant now solicitous, polite, nearly deferential to the boy whose fate Vardys quickly assessed as a potential business opportunity, whose plight Vardys translated into collateral, currency, profit in the amber merchant's deep, deep pocket. Vardys: middleman, conduit, go-between. As it turned out, the amber merchant peddled other goods as well. As it turned out, the amber merchant hawked passports out of the Pale, deals, room for one more on History's cattle ship.

"I don't have any money," Nathan said.

Vardys smiled. From the floor between his feet, he brought up to his lap a sack and removed a loaf of bread, a hunk of yellow cheese. With the knife he'd used to cut his fingernails, he sliced the bread and cheese and made a sandwich for Nathan, one for himself. "But perhaps you own something of value. A memento, perhaps, from one of your parents, an inheritance you might consider—"

"I have this," my grandfather said, hoisting himself forward. The back of his shirt was soaked and pulled away like a bandage from the wooden seat. He unbuttoned the rear pocket of his trousers and retrieved a small silk pouch, so warm it felt alive in his palm. My grandfather untied the ribbon and shook into his other hand the gold wedding ring Isaac Lieb had placed on Simca's finger in Volkovysk over sixteen years before. Their son would not have been so quick to offer the ring to Vardys if Simca and Isaac had not told him to do so as soon as they recognized the legitimacy of the amber merchant's solicitation. My grandfather's parents traveled on the light which burned through the window glass, they rode in tandem with the earthbound train, they advised discreetly in voices barely distinguishable from the clatter of wheels on track, so embedded in that cacophony were their instructions. It is unlikely that anyone but Nathan heard their voices at all.

Vardys lifted a brow in appraisal, extended his fingers like tongs with which to grasp the wedding band. My grandfather withdrew it. "You would have to explain the arrangements to me before I would pay," he said. "I would have to be . . . sure."

"You don't trust me?"

"No," said Nathan, honest where another might have been cunning. "I don't trust you."

A rush of derision rose in Vardys' chest, his mouth wide as a siphon waiting to be filled. But when he saw that Nathan's face was stricken, that the boy anguished over having to speak such a judgment, the merchant recognized his own diminishment, the tragedy of his connivances, and for a moment he was chastened. For a moment he regretted his life, that it had cost him a child's respect.

Blue earth.

My grandfather watched the miners dig amber lumps from that coastal clayish soil, neither water nor land. In a vat, Nathan rinsed clean the "blue earth" lode and piled the stones in Vardys' wooden wagon as farmers pile just-harvested vegetables into carts they pull between the furrows, as fishermen heap their catch of mackerel or carp into the boat's hold.

Some miners in boots to their hips walked into the Baltic and brought amber up in nets. Fishing for stones. My grandfather saw the nets come up flashing light, filled with rock that seemed to be squirming for breath. In Klaipeda, categories quietly collapsed—sea, ground, inert, alive—as the first forest of amber-making pines had slid into the water forty million years before, the resin that oozed from the trees' bark hardening in time, insects and animal hair and seed pods drifting to the earth entrapped forever in the strange new formations. Pagans who settled there believed that the sun itself resided in the stone. They named the calcified sunlight amber, they named their glittering country Amber Land. In Lithuania, in Amber Land, my grandfather learned from the fossils that the universe has a memory, and he listened for the buried truths that superseded the Talmud, for the laws he would not find in the Mishnah, for the knowledge mouthed by witnesses

44

locked in the rock that looked like liquid, like the tea he'd fixed for Simca in the days of her final illness, glasses and glasses of amber-colored tea. He listened for his mother in the midst of the miner's shouts, for the dirge she'd hummed to him as other mothers sang lullabies to their children. He heard her voice coming to him from the amber nugget in his pocket, the one Vardys had given him in Maier Nelkin's shop, and it seemed as if Simca herself dwelled in that tiny, translucent crypt he kept against his heart.

I am making this myth from a few facts I wear like a necklace of amber beads. Talismans. Amulets. Glasses of tea.

Say the miners taunted my grandfather. Say they ridiculed his earlocks, his narrow shoulders, his skinny legs. Say they called him names, or simply called him what he was: Jew, as if his identity carried its own curse, and they needed no further epithet with which to wound the boy from Vilnius, Vardys' boy, the Jew-boy. They knew not to touch him. Vardys had made this clear. "Lay a finger on him and I'll snap your neck like a chicken's." They believed him. They knew it was not kindness that led Vardys to his protective assertions. They recognized him rightly as a man without affections. They understood his mentality, the calculations that determined all his relations, and they wondered exactly what this Lieb boy was worth to the amber dealer, how he had computed my grandfather's value.

When they taunted Nathan, he rose above their cruelty, he floated to the tips of the pines, he thought to himself: I am not here, this is not my life. He did not recognize the words as his mother's own chant of denial in the face of her losses, her grief born again in her son as gumption, her childhood pain his power. When his sleep was sundered by dreams whose dangers continued to threaten him even as he lay awake on the pallet in

45

Vardys' kitchen, he repeated the phrases whose origins he did not know, but whose cadence comforted him as if Simca were singing: I am not here, this is not my life.

On one such morning in Klaipeda, he woke to other melodies. Through the opened window, accordion music wafted up from the sea, and a raucous male chorus sang Lithuanian lyrics, my grandfather understanding a word here and there: maiden, beautiful, kiss. Nathan was fourteen years old, and he had been exiled from joy for so long he could not remember the last time he had celebrated his life, but he recognized in the song borne to him through the darkness the pitch of pure happiness. He followed it as children were lured by Hamelin's piper, making his way from Vardys' house two miles to the water, where the singing emanated. He clambered over moon-glazed rocks, navigated through thickets of pine trees whose trunks he groped for with his stretched-out hands. Once he tripped over a twisted vine, and his cheek burned from the scrape he treated with mud that he applied like salve to his wound. What if he had forgotten to put on his shoes, so entranced was he by the melody toward which he traveled like an animal returning to its instinctual home? Then the soles of his feet would be raw from the needle-strewn earth, from the stones on his path. Yet the sting of these injuries was not enough to deter him, so drawn was he to the scene of jubilation, whose sounds had grown so resonant now that they seemed to form a protective cushion on which he could walk.

Finally, he could see the men. They had built a bonfire at the water's edge. The light from the flames reddened the sea so that the Baltic itself appeared to be burning. Burning water. Blue earth. Fishing for stones. A captor who offered deliverance. All his life my grandfather would remember Klaipeda as one remembers a dream: tolerant of its contradictions, its violations of reasons, its mysterious depths.

A dozen revelers sang and danced on the radiant shore. He could not distinguish many of their faces from the distance between their site and the clump of trees in which he hid. But when one or another of them turned to him directly at such a moment that the bonfire illumined his features, Nathan recognized miners among whom he labored, men dour by day, taciturn and wearied, now transformed, rejuvenated, ecstatic. As if Nathan's arrival functioned as some subliminal signal to the men, they began to shed their clothes, plunging nude into the water like a school of light-slicked sea creatures returning to their habitat. He had never learned to swim. He had wanted to swim in the Neris, the river that ran through Vilnius, but Simca forbade it, she was frightened he would drown, and my grandfather did not disobey that particular proscription. Perhaps he intuited how much he would love the buoyancy, the extension of vista, how swimming would become for him less a sport than a ritual, crucial to his well-being and therefore a source of constant combat between them. Sometimes he would walk to the river's edge, sit on the grass, and study the bodies gliding through the shimmer. He would feel himself one of them, his imagination entirely immersed, his identification so complete, that afterward his arms would ache from the miles he'd never swum, his skin would tingle from the water he'd never entered. Now, in the darkness, those bright mornings returned to him as the memory of true experience, and he longed to return to the state he had never enjoyed, unless it was the womb's waters he remembered, that first sea in which we all are spawned.

One by one, the miners surfaced, swam back to shore, dried off, and dressed themselves, merriment spent, the fire dying. One of them smothered the flames entirely, and then the men were shadows or less, and murmurs receding into silence, and my grandfather was alone on their abandoned beach.

47

I can see the neat pile he made of his clothes. I can see him wading into the Baltic, black now except for a ribbon of moonlight rippling over the surface. I can see him stretching out on the water—Klaipeda, the Quincy Street Y, the beaches near Boston—then propelling himself forward, my grandfather, Nathan Lieb, mastering the currents, learning endurance, laughing, laughing, laughing into the limitless dark.

5

Simca's wedding band bought her children passage on a ship leaving a German port for America. But Vardys declined to speculate how Nathan and Ruth would fare on the illegal land route from Russia to Germany, a trek for which stamina was not more vital than bribes and lies and chicanery as skillful as that of assaulting bandits, some themselves Jews, who fleeced Jews on the run.

"For an additional fee," he said, as if he were discussing grades of meat, or the difference between first- and second-class vacation accommodations, "I can put you and the girl on my brother-in-law's fishing boat right here in Klaipeda, and he'll take you across the Baltic to Hamburg. Maybe he'll even teach you how to catch a carp!"

My grandfather said, "All I have is my mother's ring."

His labor at the amber mines ended, he was packing his clothes into his satchel. From the window, a breeze rode in off the water and Nathan followed the current's passage through the room as if a bird, or some other being, were visible to him in the curtain's billow, the hanging mirror's sway, the ruffled pages of Vardys' account book opened on the raw pine table at which he worked.

Vardys stared at his charge. In the weeks he had been in this house, the boy's presence had begun to accumulate weight, anchoring itself into the rooms Vardys had never shared with anyone before. Nathan's voice and his gestures and even his silences acquired density, registered themselves on the merchant in increasing detail and dimension. As Vardys received the knowledge that relation alone provides, the most negligible domestic experiences—peeling an orange, making a bed, closing the shutters at the sign of a storm—thickened with implication he could not name.

One night he'd heard Nathan weeping, and the amber merchant had risen from his bed to stand in the shadows from which he could see but not be seen. Vardys had stood there for fifteen minutes or more, keeping watch over the child whose sniffles and sighs sounded more to him like a man's than a minor's, more like the sounds he himself might make (he did not know he knew this), were he ever to let loose the sadness that, over the years, had gathered in his chest like matter in a clogged drain. If anyone were to have asked Vardys why he'd neither silenced Nathan nor returned to his own room, what it was he was learning or protecting or waiting for at his hidden post, he would have lied: "I thought he might be having convulsions. Did I want him to die in my own house and be blamed for it?"

But in truth, Vardys suspected nothing so dire. He might have been as perplexed by his vigil as any witness to it might have been, and his relief at Nathan's regained composure resembled, if not a father's care, then at least a friend's.

My grandfather buckled the strap around his valise.

"All right!" Vardys yelled, as if in the midst of an argument. He slammed shut his account book. "All right,

49

you'll go to Hamburg on Mikhail's fishing boat regardless!"

And then he stormed through the door into the weed-tangled yard, and my grandfather heard Lithuanian curses rending the placid morning air.

Read the firsthand accounts of Europe's immigrants at the century's turn.

Absorb the litanies of loss: "We left everything and everyone behind."

In these catalogs of the journey's hardships—illnesses, storms, terror that nightmares could not contain, miscarriages and deaths and the faltering faith that is itself a kind of death—hardly a witness records the failure of nerve, the turning back, the course retraced to the more familiar pain from which these thousands fled. Into such courage I submerge myself like an orthodox woman at the mikva, a Christian being baptized, a Hindu walking into the holy Ganges. In those depths I find my story's source. Everything I know, or need to know, rises up to me from that sea.

I dream them: Nathan and Ruth dreaming the future in which I will live to dream their pasts. Under the tarp, they shared shelter with Mikhail's netted lode—a dozen fish whose last thrashings the children watched in silent affiliation, those snared carp more family to them now than this man who grunted directions at them as if they were creatures only slightly more evolved than those of his day's catch. Under the tarp, my grandfather and his sister succumbed to exhaustion and the boat's tossing and the starless sky's rain.

"The fish smell bad," Ruth whimpered into her brother's ear.

Developing in conditions of extremity a talent for aphorism that would demonstrate itself even in kinder

50

times, Nathan said, "Not as bad as we must smell to the fish."

Delivered to Hamburg like the cargo they were, the ensuing week of quarantine at least restored them to human categories. If Vardys' brother-in-law had ignored them, here in this former warehouse for ship parts they were constantly examined, questioned, instructed, and treated with an array of disinfectants, purgatives, and tonics. If the quarters were overcrowded, the food tasteless, and the German clerks brusque, at least my grandfather heard his own name and his sister's called out a dozen times a day— Lieb, Nathan! Nelkin, Ruth!—and the mattresses on which they slept at night smelled not of fish but of people like themselves, fellow emigrés, predecessors, anonymous kin leaving behind, like ancestors, the consoling proof of their prior passage through this phase of the family journey.

In his bunk, where the uneradicable odor of living flesh was as comforting to him as the perfume of his mother's cooking had been, my grandfather imagined the previous tenants of this cot and the ones to come once he had departed. He felt them all shifting about on the mattress he shared with them, siblings in a common bed, he and Ruth attached now to a large band of relations he was not supposed to know. Maier Nelkin, Vardys, Mikhail, the Hamburg clerks who oversaw this place—all of them had encouraged in him a belief in his isolation, which perhaps was his true predicament in the material world they controlled. They would have welcomed him as an initiate into their commonwealth of disappointment; they would have accepted him into their legion of the corrupted—all ties renounceable, all convictions pale, all dreams devalued as if they were the currency of a failing market.

But like his mother, Nathan Lieb resided in the territory of the spirit, where now he reclaimed the solace of camaraderie stolen from his father, who, had he lived, would have shared it with his son, this shy boy from Vilnius, no surviving relative but the half-sister in his care, my grandfather, fifteen years old, about to sail to America with the entire tribe he had discovered, hidden like contraband in the mattress on which he lay.

The hull!

Say this is the third day at sea. Well after midnight, my grandfather leaves the pallet he shares with Ruth and climbs from steerage up the laddered stairs to the deck. Water and sky have merged into a seamless miasma. The wind-whipped mist stings Nathan's cheeks. He sticks out his tongue, as children do in a snowfall, and tastes the airborne brine. Beneath him the ship tosses and groans, as if all the restless sleepers within it have become the vessel itself, a single body of which he is a pore, a hair, a line across one palm. He runs his hand along the rail, and it is like touching his own bone. Since boarding, Ruth has been curled up in the bed assigned to them deep inside the ship, where she tries to forget her terrors: Will they crash into another ship? Will they sink? Will they die on board from contaminated food? Nathan comforts her with assurances of safety and health, but in fact, here on deck in the land-vanished dark, he neither believes his assertions nor fears their failure.

Does he fear that his breathing will stop or his blood will suddenly dry up in his veins or his senses will cease to operate? He trusts this boat as he trusts his own body, which is to say he sustains for both a dream of survival, a fantasy that both passages—the boat on the ocean, his life in the world—will proceed unharmed.

In the midst of his calm, a girl screams. For a moment, he thinks her a gull or some other seabird, but then the quality of human sound that humans recognize as other animals recognize the cries of their kind registers itself on

Nathan. He runs toward the voice, which comes from the direction of the stairs he mounted, his heels slapping now against the deck's wet boards. She is pressed up against a glass-door cabinet in which a pile of deflated life rafts mock her distress. A strongly muscled man, his unbuttoned shirt flying out from his body like a rigid tail, has her pinioned there with one hand, the other yanking at the bodice of her dress.

"Let her go!" my grandfather says, his reedy voice thinned even more by his breathlessness, so that his injunction sounds like a jingle instead, and the meager force he summons with which to push against the man's attacking arm turns Nathan's would-be assault into hardly more than a nudge. But the simple fact of my grandfather's presence is enough to turn the probably drunk crewman away from the girl, whose profile, through not extraordinary, had riveted the man the moment he'd seen her board the boat in Hamburg. His lust (so much of it already rage) converts now entirely to rage, focuses on Nathan, delivers itself with one brutal blow to my grandfather's right eye.

When he comes to, the eye is swollen shut and the pain inside it so deep he fears his assailant might have plucked it out, or surely damaged it beyond repair. But Nathan manages a smile for the stunned girl he rescued, on whose lap his pummeled head now rests.

"My name is Nathan Lieb," he says. "From Vilnius."

Through his good eye, he sees her as she is, a dark-haired girl his age, her color-drained skin unblemished, her high forehead smooth as the inside of a shell, her features a harmonious natural landscape, beautiful to him in its plainness. He sees her also, simultaneously, as a child and a woman, young and aging. Her face becomes a fan on whose panels are painted all the stages of her life. My grandfather does not yet know that such visions always announce the onset of love, which exists outside of time, which encircles time as if in embrace and holds a hundred years easily in its arms. Surely, he thinks, he is the only young man in the world who has ever seen a girl in this way, and through a single eye at that. He decides that his attacker was a providential agent, whose blow released in my grandfather the power to see through one eye what other people missed with two.

Years later, long after his injury has healed and left him ordinary again, he will remember the hubris of his conviction and the sweet pain that throbbed, for the first time, not in his eye at all.

6

On Blue Hill Avenue, in the Roxbury section of Boston, my grandfather lived in a single room with his new wife and his half-sister Ruth, her space and theirs separated by a flowered chintz curtain they'd hung from a ceiling-high rod. Each morning the young immigrants, three years in America now, sat at the secondhand kitchen table on Ruth's side, poached an egg apiece on the hotplate they used as a stove, boiled the water for tea, one teabag for three cups, one sugar cube split into thirds.

Of the sounds they each had overheard during the night from the other side of the drape—the couple's muffled cries at climax, Ruth's nightmare screams—they never spoke. Silence was the one privacy they could afford, and they maintained it fastidiously, as if caring for a fancy house with rooms for everyone, many levels, thick doors and walls. Their actual quarters required economies, material and otherwise. Tight pockets, tight lips: they learned to scrimp.

After breakfast, Ruth or my grandmother Esther took the dishes in a metal basin down the hall to the bathroom they shared with the other tenants who rented rooms above a block of stores: from the butcher shop directly beneath their abode, Nathan and Esther and Ruth could hear the chickens squawking in the wooden pens where they awaited the slaughterer. The newlyweds said they barely noticed the animal noises. But Ruth hated the sounds. She tried stuffing her ears with sealing wax, but this only worked to deepen the squawks, so that the chickens seemed to bark like dogs instead.

They were not as poor as their living conditions suggested. They had jobs. At the Thomas O'Malley Hat Factory a trolley ride away, Esther and Ruth stitched bowler brims to crowns; Nathan worked in the packing room, stacking the finished hats a dozen to a box, tissue-paper wad for protection on top. They worked ten hours a day, twenty minutes for the lunch they brought from home: a sardine sandwich on dark bread, or a chicken leg from last night's soup, or pot cheese and lettuce on a roll. Small bites, long chewed. Flavor stretched as far as the future for which they saved. They banked half their salaries—as if my grandfather's business (he wasn't sure as yet what kind it would be) or the house they'd buy (here in Roxbury, Esther planned, or neighboring Dorchester) existed in fact rather than hope, and they would risk bankruptcy or foreclosure if they missed weekly payments to creditors, utilities, wholesalers.

Along with the formal English they studied in night school two evenings a week, they were learning the argot of American commerce. My grandmother took to it, as to a jazzy tune. She liked the rhythms of improvisation, the potential for surprise, the promise of a flourishing finale. Her husband went along, cooperative, dependable, but

55

lacking any of her fiery drive. If anything, his wife's ambition amused him. He called her "Mrs. Rich." Once he
sketched her wrapped in furs from head to foot, so that
only her eyes peeked through the exotic cartoon swad-
dling. His insouciance confused her at first, alarmed her
later, left her bitter at the end.

"But what do you want from life?" she said.

She meant status, possessions, a good address. She
had left behind a well-to-do family, after all, the saddles
and boots and belts her father sold in his leather-goods
store commanding high prices, regular customers. My
grandmother had come to America to escape a marriage
planned for her when she'd been five, not to relinquish
forever the comforts of a prosperous life.

My grandfather smiled. He put his hands on Esther's
shoulders as if he were a healer and she had an illness
from which he could save her, as he had saved her that
night on the ship. For two years, he'd courted her, walking
the ten blocks from his and Ruth's room to the flat Esther
shared with her cousins and their four children. Where he
had learned the rituals of romance, Nathan could not say.
He seemed to have discovered an entire bodily system,
akin to circulation, that was designed to woo.

"I want time to dream," he said, which was why he
did not mind the rote work at the factory—it left his imagination free for its own projects—and why he went about
their spartan regimen so cheerfully—it was the unclut-
tered status quo he valued, not the acquisitive future to
which Esther aspired.

Her heart dropped like a purse of coins falling through
a ripped pocket. If her husband had just given away every
penny they had saved, she could not have felt more robbed.

When he saw the dimensions of her disappointment,
he told her, "I've been thinking of a clothing store."

He knew how far his words would carry her, and he
allowed her to travel, for now, beyond the limits of his

intent. What he thought he would try, in fact, was a secondhand outlet, an inventory for which he'd have to pay little, a business of minimal profit and easy bookkeeping, refugee clothes for refugees. He found enough ironic wit in the notion to satisfy him. And the poignancy of the enterprise moved him, as if more than old garments were entailed; as if souls, asleep in the discards, waited for their next incarnations, their new lives. In a dream, he told his parents of his plan and they winked at him, all of them enjoying this little bit of mischief, this small joke on death.

My mother and her sister, Joan, were little girls when their Aunt Ruth, who lived with them, married a haberdasher from Columbus, Ohio—he had come to O'Malley's on a buying trip—and moved there with him for good. She had not been happy in Boston for so long a time. From the day Esther had joined them, Ruth had watched her brother and his new wife feud and nuzzle, finish each other's sentences, or contradict everything the other said. It did not matter to Ruth what form these interchanges took; what injured her was that Nathan had abandoned her as his primary companion, his only kin, his partner in this exile she had been so reluctant to undertake. From the moment he had encountered Esther on the ship and decided to follow her to Boston, a city he had not even heard of before, his attention had been divided as if he truly had been blinded in one eye and could not notice Ruth if Esther held his sight, as if he could only see one person at a time.

Sometimes Ruth tried to remember herself and her brother in Vilnius, when their mother was still alive, but all of Ruth's memories seemed to be buried with Simca, whose own face her daughter could barely summon. As for her father, nothing remained of him for Ruth but the fear he had always engendered in her. She could not have told you his work, his habits, the color of his hair or eyes. She knew she'd had a childhood—everybody did—yet sometimes Ruth Nelkin believed she'd sprung whole into this world aboard the ship that had brought her here from Europe, then left her stranded alone in Boston, Massachusetts, though Nathan and Esther slept no more than ten feet away.

But it was not until his sister was gone that my grandfather, himself, missed those years of a simpler fidelity than marriage or parenthood required. One night at supper he announced to Esther and their children that he was taking the train to Ohio—this would be the only trip he ever made, except for the one he'd taken halfway around the world from Lithuania—and he would bring Ruth back.

"She's a married woman," my grandmother said.

"She's my sister," he said, suggesting another pattern of loyalties.

Oh, how distinguished he would have looked, dressed in his good suit and his polished shoes, sitting in his coach erect as a rabbi, a scholar, a highly regarded attorney-at-law! A professional man of significant accomplishment on his way to a conference, perhaps, or a teaching assignment at a good midwestern college; his carriage implied such honors, such worldly responsibilities. In my grandfather's face, the gravity of mission. Who on that train would have known that he had been serious from birth, that his mother had schooled him in her womb, that his father had bequeathed his infant the radical passion that transforms the most mundane occurrence, the most banal observation, the most ordinary task into historical event?

A ragman going to visit his sister in Columbus, Ohio.

Of course she did not return to Boston with him. Of course she loved him for coming so far on her behalf. She took him on a tour of the town. She showed him the limestone State Capitol building. They walked along the Scioto River. She took him to the Park of Roses, thousands of plants in shocking bloom. On the campus of the state university on the north side of the city, they watched the

58

students hurry from building to building, or lounge on the swatches of lawn, or stroll the paths in a dazed state of reflection. Here, in the middle of America, in a city named for the first European to find the country millions of subsequent Europeans would claim as their own, my grandfather and his sister imagined themselves in Vilnius again, two children going home together, going home, together.

7

When Pa died of a sudden massive hemorrhage, my mother found in the pocket of his tattered bathrobe an ancient beetle, perfectly preserved in an amber nugget. Thirty-five years later, I hold the nugget in my hand.

"Remember him," the beetle tells me, "as I have been remembered."

My words are blood, transparent as resin, that radiant fluid the trees of the Baltic coast gave up to the earth, that plasma turned to rock, to past-bearing amber. Luminous crypts.

My words are blood, transparent as resin.

I will heal as the trees healed.

II

Flo

1

When the forties ended, my grandfather died.

I was six years old.

I was barely tall enough to see out a window to the street below. A child's grief is parochial, fiercely self-centered. I would have to grow older, see farther, before my vision incorporated his. Life is not so much a journey, perhaps, as a widening of the territory one can view from a single place. I would have to realize what it meant, for example, that every evening before the radio news came on, I watched him wrap himself in his prayer shawl and listened to him chant the *Kaddish* for all those who perished in camps in Germany and Poland during the war.

I come from a long line of mourners. There is some solace in that.

Flo's family would have been among the victims for whom my grandfather prayed. Not that he knew them. Not that her true name was Flo. In the DP camp or on the ship they finally let her board, or perhaps in that maze of regulations through which she burrowed on Ellis Island, her name got changed. Life had done so much to her already that she let it do one more thing, and she gave up her real name for this chorus girl's pseudonym she always said with some embarrassment.

I loved her labored speech, the slow formulation of a phrase like a wood carving I might be watching her whittle. She came from Poland, not far from the Lithuanian town where Pa had been born. Like him, she spoke what my American parents called "broken English," no longer the language of the elders alone, but now the tongue of scores of neighbors my parents' age and younger, even some children like myself. "Broken English." I never liked the term; it seemed to me disapproving, the rebuke one might mask for a visitor who had dropped a piece of one's china, knocked over a crystal lamp. "Broken English." As if the newcomer's words were fractured, damaged beyond repair. These people were "survivors," I learned, and from Flo I would learn what my parents tried to shield me from: who Adolf Hitler was and why he would have murdered me, or tried to, had I grown up in Europe, speaking Polish and Yiddish like Flo, her inmate number inked forever across her faintly freckled arm.

She is a dozen women, a town's worth, an entire generation of daughters scattered over the world like crumbs from History's sweaty hand.

*   *   *

Flo lived directly beneath us. She brought us an apple cake the day we arrived in Pittsburgh. "You'll play with my daughter," she said to me, as if delivering a prophecy. "You'll be like sisters." Channah was three years old, a baby really, but I did spend hours with her, shaping clay in Flo's kitchen, doing puzzles on the linoleum floor, making up games on the hallway stairs—Jumpsies, we named one, and Climbing the Mountain. Sometimes when Channah and I played, Flo would watch us transfixed, mesmerized, as if we had become the sisters she had predicted, truly kin. Sometimes, when Channah was napping or at another child's, I stayed anyhow, to visit with Flo.

Soon I was going downstairs when I was certain Channah would not be home. "I'll tell you a story," Flo would begin, and I would listen to the vivid tales of her Polish past. I would imagine myself her daughter then, all her secret knowledge passed on to me like family jewels, like heirlooms, treasures meant only for offspring. Then my mother would call me, or my father would come home from the produce yards, his feet heavy and unmistakable on the rubber-treaded stairs, and we would all be reminded of who belonged to whom.

"I think she gets lonely," my mother said. "He works all the time."

Flo's husband, Saul, a Romanian Jew, sold storm doors and windows, his territory mill and mining towns in western Pennsylvania, in Ohio, along the treacherous roads of West Virginia. Some nights he came home past midnight; some days he worked a seven-day stint. He wrote up orders during supper, he took calls from potential customers who'd seen the ads he ran in their neighborhood newspapers. Sundays I'd see him asleep in his living room chair, maps of the next week's route spread open on the floor, his traveling arrested for a moment, his constant motion briefly stalled.

65

Of her husband's pace, Flo would say, "He doesn't mind. When he's working, he forgets."

She stayed home and remembered. Memory was her work. Sometimes she sat for hours on the crewel-cushioned rocker by the bay window, its deep sill covered with plants she raised from seedlings she bought at Woolworth's to foot-high stalks and trellised vines. She dropped her gaze into that forest as if it sheltered the past itself.

"Here," she said, handing me a tiny jar. "One squeeze to each."

I filled the dropper again and again with the liquid fertilizer and fed each plant. I thought of Pa, the garden he'd grown each summer on the porch of our house in Boston, and my throat constricted, but then the muscles released, the image of my grandfather broke into minute particles, a strange dust that drifted down and disappeared into Flo's ivy, philodendron, asparagus fern. It might be days before another reminder might strike. In the first months, I had thought of him constantly, his voice like a ringing in my ears which muted all other sounds. My eyes had grown gritty, sore and red, from staring at his absence. Nights I had woken screaming, though in my dreams I was only whispering his name in the darkness of the Pullman car I rode with my mother from Boston to Pittsburgh again and again and again. Now, feeding Flo's plants, I was making myself forget him. I did not know that. I was a child, not yet seven, and the words I would learn decades later would have been gibberish to me then: trauma, grief, denial, repression. Learn them I would, in my thirties, a prayer to mouth when the recovered pain threatened to fell me, until finally the words—trauma, grief, denial, repression—broke open like seed pods and the memories inside grew into stories and novels. "Who has had the biggest influence on your development as a writer?" an interviewer asked me once, and I knew she wanted a literary mentor—I said Chekhov—but the true answer would have been Flo. For years, I listened to her tales, an oral chronicle volumes long. Who taught me more about recall? Whose stories were braver than hers?

"I give her the greatest credit," my mother liked to say. "To suffer like she did. To lose so much. To come to a strange place and start all over, with nothing. It takes a very strong person, believe me. Very strong."

"If your mother had been in the camps," Flo would tell me some years later, "she would have saved lives."

When we had been in Pittsburgh for seven months, my mother said, "Your father and I have to make a trip and you'll stay with Flo. Just for one week. You'll go to school every day like normal, and she'll make you Cream of Wheat, and I told her how you like Ritz crackers and a glass of milk at night. I bought you a new nightgown today, too. You'll sleep in Channah's room. Just like a vacation, right?"

My parents' journey and my week at Flo's had nothing to do with vacation. They were going to Boston. Aunt Joan had written, "He goes off for hours, he gets lost. The police have to bring him home in the wagon. Yesterday I found him sitting alone in the kitchen with one of my butcher knives in his hands. Sometimes he doesn't know us. God knows what goes on in his mind anymore. I cry all the time. I talked it over with Sid and we came to a decision, so tomorrow I'm calling the Jewish Home."

When he had been there a month, my mother had said to my father, "I have to see for myself. That he's happy."

"He's not happy," my father had said. "He's old. But I think we should go anyhow."

By now I had learned how to make myself numb whenever Pa's name was uttered. The news was never good. For a while I had plotted ways to rescue him from Boston myself, and I had thrown a shoe against the living room window, rehearsing how I would break into the Jewish Home and steal him away—glass sprayed all over the room, and one shard cut me just above the eye—but finally I had given up hope, which is memory's soil, and so the past and future were dying together, as if some blight had overtaken me—"chronic depression," a psychiatrist would name it years later. A few months after my parents returned from their visit to him ("When I saw him there," my mother told me recently, "I knew he was already gone"), my grandfather was dead, but how could I cry for a man who was now a stranger to me, a picture on my mother's bureau, a face I no longer recognized? Oh, it would be a long time before my parched spirit would flourish again. When it did, I would weep for my grandfather and I would weep for Flo as well, the woman who had given me refuge in her memories—"I will tell you a story, maidele"—when I was fleeing from my own.

2

In the room her two sisters shared, their bed big enough for three once she grew, she slept in the cradle her father built from Mlochini forest pine. A cabinetmaker by trade, Jacob Skolnik had his workshop in the shed behind their small house on the outskirts of Warsaw. When she was older, she would go with him to the lumber mills where he bought his wood directly from the loggers, and while her father made his purchases, she would shut her eyes and inhale the dizzying aromas of the newly split trees. She liked the swooning sensation that came over her, the limits of the solid world giving way, fluid, permeable.

Her real name was Fela. At home she was her father's helper. While her sisters Rachael and Bronia worked alongside their mother, Naomi, in the kitchen, pounding bread dough or chopping nuts or grinding meat in the iron grinder clamped to the counter's edge, Fela learned to saw and plane and hammer, her little hands callused, her fingernails torn, her arms growing muscled as a man's. Her sisters teased her—"You think you're a boy! You think you're a boy!"—and her mother worried over the failure of her youngest to master the skills of a homemaker, but Jacob said, "Should I be deprived of the companionship of a child because we happen to have had daughters instead of sons?" and Naomi could not counter the logic of such an appeal.

Fela did not mind being different. Who was not? She had never accepted the notion that a person's life was contained in the definitions of category. Child, female, Jewish, Polish—they each seemed to her like valises too small to hold the properties of any one nature, so that one was forced to jam one's being into those cramped boxes and lug them along wherever one went. If she tried to trace the origins of her conviction, she went back to her infancy, though later, in America, her husband hooted at her insistence that she could remember the first weeks of her life. She did. She remembered her mother bragging to a neighbor, "Three weeks old and she sleeps through the night!" when actually Fela lay awake in her cradle, listening to the voices of her sisters' dreams, those murmurs that rise from all sleeping forms, and she learned in those earliest days how we each speak a private language, complex and vivid as any social grammar, but untranslatable. In those vocabularies, our true beings reside, singular and free.

Like her sisters, she went to a school for Jewish girls,

but while Bronia and Rachael finished their educations when they turned fourteen and entered full-time their domestic apprenticeships under their mother's rigorous tutelage, Fela passed the examination for entrance into a Warsaw gymnasium and announced that she was also going on to the university, and then to medical school, she hoped in Vienna, where a Dr. Freud was publishing his astounding papers that confirmed the informal research she herself had been conducting since those attentive nights of her infancy. Jacob pretended dismay at his daughter's unconventional ambitions, but she could see her father's approval in the way he bounced ever so slightly in his chair, his excitement for her an energy he could barely contain. Perhaps a man who worked directly with elemental materials could never give primacy to social forms, historical idiosyncrasies, arbitrary codes that changed with time. Hadn't he and Naomi both departed from the orthodoxies of their own parents? Didn't they consider themselves modern people, Jews comfortable enough with their gentile neighbors, the insular world of their childhood shtetls forsaken for a more eclectic society, a less fearful existence? Now Fela found the notions of her own parents restrictive, and Jacob feigned a brief resistance against which his daughter could struggle.

To her mother, who would not yield, Fela announced, "This is the twentieth century!"

The following week, the Skolniks' baby girl boarded the 5 A.M. train to Warsaw. She would return twelve hours later, in time for supper. She was fourteen years old. This was the year A.D. 1938, if one used the calendar of Western civilization.

From the station in Warsaw, Fela walked five blocks along the Vistula River, then three more blocks down the street to the Pilsudski Gymnasium for Girls. The air that morning was so calm that the river's surface looked like a skin of glass or the translucent pastry dough her mother rolled, then picked up without a single rip from her floured board. Fela passed the city park where her family came in the summer for picnics, she and her sisters each allotted one piece of bread with which to feed the ducks in the pond, or the pigeons waddling over the grass like processions of uncles dressed in Shabbos suits and headed for shul. Away from her family for the first time, their presences emerged wherever Fela looked, and if she stood still and closed her eyes, she saw their faces with such clarity she could have counted the number of teeth they showed when they smiled.

At the school's front doors, propped open by wooden milk crates, a motherly looking woman directed the girls to the left or the right, new students assembling in the cafeteria, the others in in the auditorium. Fela followed the signs leading her through the corridors, photographs of Polish heroes—Chopin, Paderewski, General Pilsudski, for whom the school was named—displayed in gilt frames on the glossy walls. She was dressed like all the other girls—her father had taken her to the department store to purchase the regulation uniform, white middy and pleated gray skirt—yet it was clear to Fela, passing her eyes over the dozens of students seated on the benches at the planked tables, that she was the only Jewess among them. Even the few with dark hair had features clearly gentile. Well, wasn't it an honor, then, to be the only Jewish girl selected for entrance to the Pilsudski Gymnasium for the school year 1938–1939?

History lesson:

September 1, 1939: Germany invades Poland.
October 3, 1940: On Rosh Hashanah, the Jewish New Year, 240,000 Jews are consigned to one hundred city blocks in Warsaw, and the Nazis officially establish the Warsaw Ghetto.

71

October 16, 1940: The still-dispersed 140,000 Polish Jews, including the Skolnik family, are ordered to join immediately those already in the ghetto.

November 15, 1940: Suddenly, and without warning, with bricks and barbed wire, the ghetto is sealed. Nearly half a million people, including the Skolnik family, discover that morning that the world has diminished to one tiny corner of Warsaw, the rest of the planet breaking off and disappearing into space, for all the connection the Jews of Poland have to this earth anymore.

Bibliography:
Photographs, salvaged diaries, smuggled-out letters, oral histories, written histories, depositions, courtroom testimony, plays and poems and films, murals, friezes, sketches, lithographs, woodcuts, cantatas for the dead.

Footnote:
Fela lived, and Rachael.

About her family's life in the ghetto, about their deportation, about those years in Auschwitz whose horrors I have investigated with a compulsion some might call morbid, but which I consider its opposite—the spirit takes its measure, I find, strengthens itself, extends itself out of the self, adopts the dead that instant before their deaths, rescues, as it were, their beings, retrieves, as it were, their light—of all that pain, Flo said only, "We suffered very much." The anecdotal recitation was suspended, the details not so much withheld as left to me to discover (I would understand this many years later), she having brought me to the point in the world's history where conventional narrative no longer suffices, where language falters, defers to the silence in which a new alphabet struggles to form itself under the bone pits, under the eyeglass mounds. Hieroglyphs multiply in the ash-fed earth.

How did the sisters survive? Girls sixteen and nineteen, the strong-willed student and the housewife manqué, for what new roles did the commandant tap these two?

Bearing in her face her intelligence as if it were her most prominent feature, perhaps Fela, this serious pupil, was recruited for the Children's House, her credentials deemed "in order," a Jewish teacher for German children. Perhaps Rachael, famous for her breads and for apricot preserves her father used to sneak from the jar by the spoonful, perhaps her culinary reputation revealed itself somehow to her captor, who made her his personal cook or installed her, at least, in another kitchen in the compound, far enough away from the crematoriums so that the food she prepared would not be tainted by the smell of that particular smoke.

Or perhaps the girls' assignments were less pristine.

Perhaps they lived together in the camp hospital, subjects for experiments, fevers induced, bacteria injected, illness after illness created and cured; between sieges, a week allotted to build back strength, the semblance of health, and then the next assault.

Perhaps the commandant, seeing Rachael naked during one of his expeditions to the building where new female prisoners were stripped and shorn and assigned the uniforms that would be, for most of them, their shrouds, perhaps he was taken with the curve of her back as she lifted the camisole over her head. Perhaps he forced her to become his whore, Naomi and Jacob Skolnik's oldest daughter kept in the secret bedroom behind the door the commandant's wife believed to be a locked supply closet in his office.

Perhaps Fela, her carpentry skills disclosed, joined the

crew that built the scaffoldings on which the daily hangings in the camp took place.

(You can see that my research has been extensive. You can see the sort of data I have accumulated.)

Perhaps the girls received no special assignments at all. Perhaps others died, and they lived, for no more understandable reason than thousands of babies were murdered in Europe at the same time that I slept in the sun in my carriage in Boston's Franklin Park while my Lithuanian grandfather fed the pigeons that strolled across the American grass.

Perhaps the sisters found some way to keep each other alive, developed between them certain rituals—a particular handclasp upon arriving and at night, before they fell into the few hours of stupor still named sleep; a secret word whispered into the other's ear, as lovers murmur the syllables only they two understand, as mothers sing to their babies the song that lulls no other child into dream; a daily exchange of food, morsel for morsel, crumb for crumb, a drop of water placed by each upon the other's tongue.

A touch, a word, the semblance of food. With such small gifts we sustain ourselves, the receiving no more crucial than the offering.

3

Flo's Saul loved things.

Things were the material proof of his growing success in America. He had men working for him now. He had a telephone answering service. He had printed business cards: SAUL AND SONS HOME IMPROVEMENT CORPORATION. He did not have sons, but he invented them for business purposes; people liked to deal with family firms, he said, they trusted blood. He claimed he used his first name because it was easier to say than Teplitsky and because it came from the Bible, which gave it authority, dignity, an aura of reliability. He did not consider such reasoning dishonest. He did not think of himself as a finagler. He understood marketing, he said. He knew people. "You're the one who reads all the psychology books," he might have told Flo, if she had taken issue with his various dissemblings. "You're the one who studies behaving."

I do not know the degree to which they were at odds. I recognized her as a lonely person, but this had less to do with the life she lived now as Saul's wife than with the life she had lost in Poland, and I doubt that any husband could have compensated her for that sorrow. Still, Saul's appetite for fiscal adventures, his elevation of shrewdness to a nearly saintly attribute, must have contributed to her sense of dislocation—how different he was from her craftsman father, her domestic artist of a mother!—and paradoxically heightened her desire to preserve in America the simplicity of her parents' ways.

So Saul filled the apartment with modern gadgets that Flo ignored when he was not around.

She swept their carpets with a broom, the Hoover stashed in the coat closet where I hung my jacket when I came to visit. He bought her a Mixmaster, but she used a fork to beat her cake batters free of the last floury lump. When the landlord installed a Sears automatic washer in the basement for the tenants, Flo asked him to leave the wringer washer hooked up beside it. "In case the new one breaks," she said, "for insurance." In fact, she liked to pull each item through the rotating cylinders—her family's clothing, pillowcases and sheets, the tablecloths she pressed free of the tiniest wrinkle—each piece restored for use again in her hands.

And what of the aborted studies in Vienna, the grand ambitions to follow Freud? If she grieved for her vanquished vocation, it was not apparent. She talked of those plans with a kind of bemused and tender nostalgia, as if they had been the silly fantasies of a child, not a precocious intellect's self-avowal. Perhaps it was her reading that kept her from bitterness—sometimes when I myself am lost in a book, the words slip away from me for a moment and I am aware of my body half reclining, half sitting on the sofa, an elbow the fixed axis on which my flesh-housed mind traverses, my posture exactly like Flo's, so that it seems I have absorbed from her this specific relation to language and space, this definitive bearing in the world. Books were always piled beside her bed, on the coffee table, sometimes on the kitchen counter, so that I wondered if she read even as she washed the dishes or stirred the barley soup, a jar of which I always carried home. During her first year in America, she had devoted herself to learning English: she subscribed to *Reader's Digest* and saved in a shoebox each month's page of "It Pays to Increase Your Word Power"; she carried a dictionary in her purse and studied it at bus stops, doctors' offices, at night before she went to sleep and in the morning while the coffee perked; she bought a set of flash cards meant for children and tested herself as rigorously as she would her own daughter once Channah entered school. Soon Flo had mastered on the page the language whose words still stymied her tongue.

Beyond books, what did she study? Her past, of course, its dramas shaped and reshaped with a writerly attention to motif, to tone, to point of view. But do not think of Flo as a *hausfrau* whose repetitious labors belied a rich interior life. The work itself had power for Flo. The quotidian resonated. The simplest skills constituted for her a meta-physics. What was psychology, after all, but the science of gesture and routine? Hadn't Freud, after all, found his laboratory in "everyday life"? Was it not "everyday life" that the Nazis had tried to vanquish, destroying whole communities of people going about their unremarkable business? In their memory, she would sweep with a broom, and mix with a fork, and hang on a clothesline each garment she pulled through the wringers of the old, old machine.

Rachael was not a memory. After the war, she had returned to Poland. Flo wrote her letters on airmail paper and saved the ones from Rachael in a hand-carved mahogany lap desk that reminded her of their father. At the end of each month, Flo sent Rachael a package of clothing: warm underwear, support hose, sweaters, shirts, and neckties for her husband, a bureau chief in the sanitation department of the city of Warsaw. The goods came from neighbors like us; my mother used to save discards from our wardrobes for the Veterans of Foreign Wars Consignment Shop, but now the laundry bag that hung on the back of my bedroom door held donations to Flo's sister, who lived, my mother said, "behind the Iron Curtain," which I believed existed, an impermeable steel drape stretched from Germany to Italy, Europe's length marked by this forbidding construction of immobile pleats.

My mother imagined Rachael a prisoner of the regime, Flo's monthly cartons not unlike the packages one might send to a relative in jail. In fact, both Rachael and her husband were dedicated members of the Communist Party, and Rachael's letters to her Americanized sister always contained a paragraph praising Poland's "courageous response to Hitler's fascism," Flo translating for me in a parody of her sister's earnestness.

77

"I don't believe in God," she'd say of herself, "and I don't believe in politics either."

Once I asked her what she did believe in. She had just taken from the oven an apple cake and two loaves of rye. She broke the heel off of one loaf. "Bread," she said, handing me the steaming piece. "I believe in bread."

I knew enough about irony to understand that food was not a faith, enough about faith to know that it resided in the invisible. Yet Flo's declaration was not entirely flippant, or else what she had intended as wisecrack revealed itself to her as wise, and she sobered. I took a warm morsel into my mouth. I imagined myself a Catholic like Mary O'Hara, who came to school with ashes staining her forehead and from whose marked skin I had not been able to take my eyes. Perhaps now I, too, was tasting transubstantiation, Flo's kitchen the sanctuary, her table the altar at which communion worked for the first time its holy magic on me.

"Poland is not a place for Jews anymore," Flo said, talking still about her sister but also waking me from the dream of Christian revelation, withdrawing from that bread its forbidden iconographic power. With a knife, she cleaved the loaf in half, restoring its materiality, God turned again into the Eternal Puzzle for which no worldly proof exists.

In a clean cotton dish towel, she wrapped up the portion. "Enjoy it for supper," she instructed, and I bore home the offering, a simple gift, only itself, and yet the still-warm dough seemed to pulse in my hands like a living thing.

My mother said, "Maybe you'd like to bring a school friend home for lunch tomorrow. This would make nice sandwiches, tuna maybe, or I could—"

"No, thanks," I said, dashing her hopes yet again that I might choose for myself what she called "a normal childhood," as if it were a country to which we could move, a

78

destination at which the will could arrive on its own momentum.

In the summer of 1959, three months before the grandfatherly Russian leader, Nikita Khrushchev, visited America, Rachael wrote Flo, *All these years we carried communism like a beloved baby in our arms, and now we discover the baby has all along been dead.*

For days, Flo read the letter over and over. She read it aloud to Saul and Channah, to my parents, to me, to neighbors up and down the block. When she did her shopping, she carried the letter in her purse, and while the butcher wrapped the bones he'd saved her for soup, she read it to him. She read it to the grocer as he rang up her order, and she read it to the baker as he bagged six Danish, prune-filled and plain. At the doctor's, she read her sister's letter to the nurse who pumped tight the blood pressure cuff around Flo's arm. She read it to Channah's teacher on Parent Visiting Night. But what could any of us do? "Am I a politician?" Saul cried. "Do I look like Adlai Stevenson?"

Another letter came, this one hand-delivered by a Pittsburgh priest who had just returned from a diocesan tour of Polish shrines, Prime Minister Gomulka himself welcoming the clerics at the airport. Her husband fired, the lease on their apartment revoked, the couple living now with friends who awaited their own eviction for "Zionist sympathies," Rachael wrote, *Help us to get out of here.*

"Would you like me to pray for your sister?" the priest might have asked Flo.

"I want you to forge her a passport!" She shook her fist in his face. "I want you to deliver a bribe!"

He promised a special mass and went home to his parish. That night he would show the Ladies' Auxiliary the slides he had taken on his trip.

* * *

She was writing her own letters now: good bond paper, watermarked, a new fountain pen with extra-fine point.

"How do you call him in English who is wanting to be elected?"

"A candidate," I said.

"Dear Candidate John F. Kennedy," she read from the page she had just composed, *"I am asking you for help."*

"What about the Pope?" Saul said. Pretending to be hungry, he had been wandering in and out of the kitchen where Flo conducted her campaign. "I'm sure he'll see the name 'Flo Teplitsky' and put everything else aside."

"Thank you very much for the suggestion," Flo said. "I'll put him on my list."

Saul pulled a kitchen chair next to the one I sat on. Secretary, aide-de-camp, courier, I had spent days looking up addresses, checking her spelling, advising her on strategies of grammar and syntax, and dropping her finished letters in the mailbox. He scooped up the pile of envelopes already sealed and stamped. *"Eleanor Roosevelt,"* he read. He rolled his eyes. "Dr. Jonas Salk. Ed Sullivan." He spoke to me as if Flo were absent. "What does she think, Ed Sullivan will put her on television and let her talk to America? America cares about one Jewish woman in Warsaw? America didn't care for six million, now it will care for one?"

Flo got form letters, somewhat like sympathy cards, grimly polite and politely grim. She got referrals: undersecretaries, legislative aides, journalists who might pursue the story of Rachael's "situation." She got two tickets to "The Ed Sullivan Show," live from New York City every Sunday night.

When it seemed she had exhausted every contact, obvious and absurd, when the most she could hope for was months or years of red tape, stalls, reasons that made no sense,

Fela Skolnik Teplitsky, also known as Flo, announced defeat. "I give up," is what she said, but her fingers drummed on the table or her foot tapped against the floor. Her body's continuing momentum contradicted surrender. Where was the stoop of resignation, the downhearted shrug, the hands folded meekly in the lap? "I give up," is what she said, but I did not believe her.

On the morning of the day that Nikita Khrushchev's motorcade would pass through our neighborhood, Flo was helping my mother tie up the sagging springs of our sofa. With great exertion, they had laid it on its back, its front casters in the air like the feet of an upended turtle. It was a heavy piece of furniture, bulky and plain. "We can't afford fancy," my mother would say, admitting her preference for the delicate and ornate, resigning herself to the serviceable. But in this position, the sofa looked strangely fragile. My mother had pried the staples free from the taut fabric that covered the underside, and now the innards were exposed. Flo got down on her knees, reached in, and examined like a surgeon. "Very bad shape," she said of the springs; she could have been speaking of arteries, valves, collapsed lungs. My mother handed her lengths of twine.

"What time are we leaving?" I said. I had just finished a game of Scrabble with Channah. It was eleven o'clock. Khrushchev's motorcade was due at noon. From my bedroom window, I had looked through the stand of poplars to Murray Avenue, "the main drag," two miles of plank-floored family-owned shops in which the community's business, commercial and otherwise, transpired. Had we believed in fortune-tellers then, in storefront parlors draped in purple velveteen and filled with replicas of real antiques, gypsies would have sold us the future at the bargain rates of day-old bagels, dented cans. But given the past, centuries of bad news, who would have paid a penny for glimpses of tomorrow?

Along the parade route, knots of people gathered—
we know the human form however vague distance renders
it—these early-assembled spectators claiming curbside spots.
My tenth-grade history teacher had mandated her students' attendance—Khrushchev's coming had canceled
school—and she expected reports filled with vivid details,
eyewitnessed scenes. "Keep your eyes and ears open,"
Mrs. Floyd had directed. "Like a journalist. Be ready for
surprise."

Flo tied a final knot. "In five minutes we'll be ready,"
she said.

My mother restapled the cloth across the salvaged
springs. Channah and I helped the women right the sofa.
We pushed it back against the wall. I laid the cushions
down and stretched out on them. Nothing squeaked or
sagged beneath my weight. "It's like new," I said.

"Golden hands," my mother said, squeezing Flo's.

Who wanted to go out into the raw wind? Who wanted
to gawk at a rude Russian in a limousine? But we put on
our coats, my mother took an umbrella "just in case," and
we fell in behind the others climbing the steep hill.

At the corner we'd chosen as our vantage point, a
television crew was setting up cameras on the sidewalk,
roping off twenty feet for "Eyewitness News" machinery
and chalking an X on the spot from which the reporter
would speak. It was nearly noon.

"Maybe we'll be interviewed," my mother said.

She relished celebrity, the possibilities of transforming
fame. In the beauty parlor, she read movie magazines,
following the lives of Judy Garland, Elizabeth Taylor, the
three Gabors, as if they were relatives, as if their destinies
had anything at all to do with ours. She would have loved
to have groomed me for the stage, or a Hollywood career,
her years of effort redeemed by my stardom, the spotlight
embracing us both.

"I should tell them you're an 'A' student," she said,

as if scholarship were a substitute for livelier talents, as if the hours I spent alone in my room, reading, wrapped in silence, prepared me in any way for a talky television debut.

I slipped my arm like a handcuff through the straps of her pocketbook and anchored her to me. "Don't you dare."

My mother laughed. "A person would think I suggested Siberia." She turned to the space on her other side, where Flo stood, in order to share the joke, I suppose, but Flo put a silencing finger to her lips and pointed with her other hand to the phalanx of motorcycles, policemen astride, moving toward us as if in invasion. Now the sirens rose. Pomp and disaster: they sound the same.

Delacroix could have painted the scene: the tidy storefronts festooned with hand-lettered signs, still-life windows framing pyramids of apples and pears, glazed breads, freshly killed chickens and egg cartons stacked beneath the sacrificial birds.

After the motorcycles, and the mayor's car, and a squadron of high-stepping majorettes, the nose of the limousine crested the hill and began its slow passage down seven crowd-bordered blocks, a clatter of applause traveling like static in the air through which the Lincoln moved.

Nikita Khrushchev. I remember his face as clearly as if I had seen him only a day ago, but twenty-five years have passed by since I looked into those rheumy eyes, their brightness nearly buried in the fleshy pillows of his cheeks. "It's him," Channah said. He was grinning; I saw the gap between his front teeth, the mole by his flat nose. An aging cherub, a wrinkled imp. Where was that malice I knew I should fear? "We will bury you." Wasn't that the promise he'd made? I wanted to talk him out of his threats. I wanted to make an appeal to him. I wanted the procession to come to a dead stop. I wanted the momentum of that hearselike limousine arrested, the driver throwing his ignition key to the ground, the famous passenger disembarking, History itself halted in its tracks.

But it was not because of me that the uniformed chauffeur braked. Who can understand fate's orchestrations? From the empty poultry crates banked against the butcher shop, a swirl of white feathers blizzarded upward in a rush of wind. As if that sudden earth-sprung squall were a sign for which she'd waited, Flo flew through the spiraling chicken down into the street and flung herself across the hood of Khrushchev's car. That action seemed to end all others in its midst, stealing its energy from whatever moved or breathed or uttered sound. Wheels, hearts, mouths in mid-word: all stilled, immobilized. Out of that stasis, Flo's voice rang. "Give me my sister!" she screamed in Yiddish, even as the Secret Service men descended on her, even as they manacled her hands and her feet, even as they carried her like a trussed bird to the paddy wagon. "Give me my sister! Give me my sister!"

All the sirens in the world could not silence that much pain.

4

Saul said she was suffering from "exhaustion." He said she was "getting a good rest." He said she needed "peace and quiet" and "a little time to herself" and "a place to relax."

"You'd think she was on a cruise, the way he talks,"

84

my mother said. "What that poor woman must be going through."

"What is she going through?" I asked. My stomach quaked; my tongue tasted like a tarnished spoon.

My mother said, "It's nothing to talk about, believe me."

She sighed. For my mother, a sigh was the proper repository for all that was grim and awful in life. Sighs were utterances emptied of etymology, hollow as coffins into which the tragic could be consigned. When she said, "It's nothing to talk about, believe me," perhaps she meant that words revealed too little, rather than too much. Perhaps she was not the censor I took her to be.

But I wanted more than Saul's euphemisms and my mother's mute sadness. Channah refused even to admit that her mother was in a hospital at all, let alone Western Psychiatric, on the outskirts of Pittsburgh. Flo was in Albany, New York, Channah said, visiting cousins. Flo was in Tucson, Arizona, staying at a spa. Flo was in Tel Aviv, where Rachael would arrive "any day," her visa secured by her sister's heroic appeal to Khrushchev during his historic visit here. I allowed Channah the refuge of her lies, but for me fantasy offered no solace. Was she still screaming? Would she get better? Did she remember me, or anyone, at all?

I sent her letters and poems and cartoons I clipped from the *Pittsburgh Press*. I sent her homemade cards and store-bought ones, including a giant fifty-cent Hallmark festooned with ribbons and embossed gold lettering and life-size roses printed on the parchment stock. *Get well soon*, the verses implored, and *Thinking of you*, and *Hope you'll soon be up and around*.

Weeks passed without acknowledgment.

"Maybe I'll visit her," I said.

My mother blanched. "It's not the kind of hospital for

visiting. Saul and Channah are the only ones allowed," she said, reminding me whose kin I was, and wasn't. But then she flushed, ashamed of her jealousy, embarrassed to have me witness it. She hugged me to her. "You have always been a very sympathetic type of child. In Boston, you used to cry every time you saw your grandmother, may she rest in peace, give herself her insulin injections. 'Don't hurt, Nana, don't hurt!' Such tears—you would have thought you were watching her cut off her arm."

My mother seldom mentioned my life in Boston. I think we were in a kind of collusion; whatever I forgot blunted her own memories, my amnesia a film of gauze she could lay across her own jagged wounds, from which I would then be shielded. Once I had come upon her sobbing on her bed not long after she had visited Pa in the Jewish Home. "Go away," she had admonished me, as if sorrow were an illness I could catch by coming too close to her. "I don't want you to see me like this." She had cried like that on the night train we had taken to Pittsburgh from Boston, probably believing that the sounds she made were swallowed up by the train's noise, and I had lain in the bunk beneath her, in that roaring dark, willing her my comfort through the mattress above my head. "You have always been a very sympathetic type of child," she was saying now, more than ten years after that night-long ride, Pa weeping on the platform, his image traveling like a stowaway with me toward that foreign city where my father waited, happily, for his daughter and his wife. At sixteen, I no longer remembered that journey, or the grandparents for whom I could not bear to grieve. When my mother claimed I had suffered for Nana, I believed her in the way I believed a history teacher relating a fact about a time in which I had never lived. Still, the litany moved me—"Don't hurt, Nana, don't hurt!"—and I did not so much hear the words from my mother as feel them form again within me, and I offered them up in the present: Don't hurt, Flo, don't hurt.

But I had done nothing for Nana's diabetes, and what cure could I offer Flo's injured spirit? Only the messages I mailed her, and the one I murmured—"Don't hurt, Flo, don't hurt!"—like a prayer, or a prescription, or the warning printed on a bottle of poison, or an angry injunction forbidding further pain. For doesn't the most "sympathetic type of child" rage at the adult who deserts her? Don't we even hate the dead for leaving us behind?

She came home on a Sunday, the weather unseasonably warm, birds about to migrate confused by the balminess. "False summer," we called it, but what was false about the eighty-degree temperatures and the oceanic sky and the occasional daffodil surfacing through a mound of dead leaves? The gloomy Pittsburgh fall had given way to sunny splendor, and the city seemed less a factory town than a resort, Flo's return a festive holiday which all the coatless vacationers would celebrate.

My parents did not share my vision of a communal welcome, the Teplitskys' front door ballroom-bedecked, a sign of foot-high letters greeting Flo—"We love you!" the crayoned words would say, the whole street arriving with cakes and casseroles and Jell-O molds, a banquet assembled on the kitchen table where I had watched her all those years making her sacred bread.

My mother said, "What she needs is quiet."

"Privacy," said my father. "After all."

They exchanged the glance with which they reminded each other that no matter how tall I had grown in the last year, I was still a child they needed to shepherd into the provinces of adult life.

"I'll tell you what," my father said. "We'll take a drive to Monroeville and look at the model homes."

I did not want to spend the day traipsing through foyer after foyer, acres of broadloom, antiseptic kitchens, and a whole forest of knotty pine paneling.

"You two go," I said. "I'll read."

"It's a beautiful morning," my mother said. "Why would you coop yourself up on a day like this?"

On a day like this, I did not want to ride fifteen miles to a treeless tract. I had waited nearly two months for this day, and I would find some way to mark Flo's return, even if that amounted to nothing more than being at my window when she got out of Saul's new four-door Mercury and walked to the front door carefully, very carefully, as if the ground were covered with ice. Let my American parents tour the uninhabited "dream houses" in which the past had vanished like the city's soot. In History's neighborhood, Fela Skolnik Teplitsky was coming home from yet another exile, and I would salute her. I would salute.

5

That winter they moved to Phoenix, Arizona. "In twenty years, all you'll hear about is central air," Saul had said, returned a prophet of the marketplace after a week in the desert city looking for work. A firm there— Aladdin Cooling Specialists, Inc.—had made him an offer: selling for six months, regional manager once he knew the locale. He'd accepted on the spot, knowing he'd leave them in a year or two. Saul and Sons Home Air Conditioning Corp. He'd already envisioned the embossed business cards, the igloo motif in the upper left-hand corners.

Did Flo want to leave Pittsburgh? I couldn't tell. We hardly saw each other those months following her hospital stay. She slept late in the afternoons, the hours after school I'd once counted as my time with her. On weekends, Saul and Channah guarded her as if she were still on the ward and they were staff, charged with her care. She didn't come to our apartment at all or go to anyone else's. When I did manage brief visits with her, she spoke with such effort, it was as if her words were embedded in a viscous jell from which each syllable had to be pried. Years later, I would understand that medication—tranquilizers or antidepressants—had slowed her speech, distorted it, so that for me now, too, her English was "broken," and its foreignness alarmed me, coming as it did from that region to which we all fear banishment.

"You'll come to visit on your vacation," she managed, and the effort it took her to utter that sentence seemed to me then to belie its intent. She looked like a woman in the throes of a memory, not a woman living in the present, making plans for the future. Though she was inviting me to Phoenix, I felt she had already given me up, mourned me, and now she was remembering me even as I stood in her midst. I had grown smaller and smaller to her, as if I had been on a train that had pulled away from the platform on which she had stood, watching me disappear.

"Oh, sure," I said. "I'll come."

She did not seem to hear me, but how could she? We were already lost to each other. A familiar sadness I could not name shook me, my head roared, and I had to hold on to the table to keep from falling to the kitchen linoleum Flo had just finished scrubbing on her hands and knees.

The week that she moved, I fainted in the bathroom and my father had to carry me, like a small child, to the sofa. While we waited for the doctor, the room circled me.

89

"Middle ear infection," the doctor told us. "She's lost her sense of balance. She'll have to lie flat in bed for ten days, then another week at home to get back her strength."

In dreams, dizzied, I stumbled after her, collapsed, struggled to stand, collapsed again. Finally I gave up the effort. Then the nights passed blankly, and during the days I stopped listening for sounds of Flo in the now-vacant rooms beneath me. The doctor came and looked into my ears. "All clear," he said, more right than he knew: she was gone.

I have never been to Phoenix, Arizona. I would have to read about it in a Fodor's Guide, or an America-on-Five-Dollars-a-Day book. From the photographs she sent in the few letters we received, they lived in a suburb not unlike the ones in Pittsburgh whose model homes my parents visited so many Sundays of my girlhood there. Some cacti grew in the Teplitskys' front yard, and another exotic shrub whose name I do not know, but whose orange flowers blazed beside the carport protecting Saul's new car. In one picture, Flo and Channah pose together *on the foothills leading to the Superstition Mountains*, the inscription reads on the back in Flo's block print. Did she like it there, in her new home in the desert? In the pictures, her smile seems not so much forced as weary, the most she can muster. But who can say that she wouldn't have been sadder if they hadn't moved? The scientists testify: sunshine counters depression.

Does it counter grief? Rachael died. We heard the news third-hand, or fourth. Saul had called a cousin here, the cousin bought her bread from the same bakery where my mother shopped, the longtime clerk passed the news to her. "Heart," my mother told us. "One, two, three."

We sent Flo a sympathy card and a potted plant. I wanted to send her something from myself. At the five-

and-dime, I bought a stamp-sized lavender sachet, the kind meant to be carried in purses, two tiny squares of lace-edged satin filled with dried aromatic flowers, but I never mailed it. Instead, I put it in the dresser drawer where I kept my knee socks and anklets, and after a while I grew confused about whether I had gotten the sachet for Flo or she had sent it to me from Phoenix. I can never smell lavender wtihout thinking of Flo, as if she had worn a perfume of that scent. She didn't. She used Coty's dusting powder and sometimes a toilet water called Lemon Splash.

Say it is morning in Phoenix, Arizona. Say Flo is working in her sun-filled kitchen, all the countertops white Formica, electric range and a self-defrosting refrigerator with a freezer top. No more pans of hot water melting the encrusted ice. Say she is washing the floor on her hands and knees, one of the few old-fashioned labors she can preserve in this up-to-date "house of tomorrow," the brochures read, and the ads in the Sunday real estate section. On the radio, the "Breakfast Club" regulars banter like friends stopped in for coffee. Channah at school, Saul calling on customers; Flo does not expect the doorbell to ring. She knows her neighbors but has not taken to visiting with them, and surely no one here is on a drop-in basis with her. "She was never a mixer," my mother would say, which is true, but in the Phoenix I imagine, Flo thinks of the yard that skirts the house as a moat, across which she lowers the footbridge for Channah and Saul and which she herself rarely traverses when she is home alone. She rises, wipes her hands on the turkish towel that hangs beside the sink, walks through the oddly bright rooms—when has she ever lived in such brightness?—and peers through the front door's peephole at the mailman's face.

She opens the door.

"Mrs. Fela Teplitsky?"

"Speaking," she says, confused, as if answering the telephone.

He is a skinny man, tanned to rubber.

"You have to sign for this letter," he says. "It come registered."

She writes her name on the sheet on the clipboard he hands her, the pen attached to it with a long piece of string. Others have signed, she sees; a half-dozen names and addresses precede the line she fills.

"What is this 'registered'?" she says. "I never got mail 'registered' before."

He takes back his clipboard, gives her the letter. "It means they paid to have me deliver it."

"It comes from Poland," she says.

"You have people there?"

In her hand the letter throbs. Or is it her own pulse, rattling the parchment? "A sister," Flo says. Already she is shutting the door. "The rest are dead."

What did she do when she read the news? ("Heart," my mother said. "One, two, three.") Did she wail for hours, did she sink into a stupor? Once I dreamed she called a taxi. She tells the driver, "I would like to go to the foothills of the Superstition Mountains," and he nods. She leaves the world of houses, the horizon a grid of roof-mounted antennas through which she glimpses a fractured sky. She rides out of the maze of cul-de-sacs and streets named for trees that do not grow in this terrain: Oak Drive, Maple Lane, Blue Spruce Road. She passes the windowless shopping malls, their acres of cars like petrified cattle in cement fields. Gradually, gradually, the land reclaims itself, the sky opens an unbroken span to her, the animals who live in the brush welcome her into their country.

"Thank you very much," Flo says to the driver. "I will get out here."

"There's nothing here, lady. This is the middle of nowhere."

"How much is the fare, please?" Flo says.

He stops the cab. "Someone's meeting you here, right?"

"I am the last one," she says. She hands him the money through the glass partition that separates the front seat from the back. He blinks. Is she a dream?

When the taxi disappears, nothing remains to remind her of the old world. Far ahead, the Superstition Mountains rise like memory, the sun a radiant compass affixed to one peak. She sets out on the long trek, Fela Skolnik Teplitsky, my lost teacher, a refugee in the middle of nowhere, a grief-borne woman going home.

III

Daniel

1

When we learned that Flo's sister had died,
I walked with my mother to Rock's Florists, and we studied
the catalog of plants we could wire to Phoenix. Finally we
chose an assortment of succulents in a white ceramic bas-
ket, and while my mother paid the clerk, I wandered to
the display area in the front of the shop. On felt-covered
risers, cut-glass vases brimmed with peonies, roses, glad-
ioli, and carnations; mums grew in clay pots, pothos vines
and philodendron twined down the decorative steps, and
overhead, the mossy fronds of huge asparagus ferns brushed
my hair. I thought of Flo's plants, how reverently she had

tended them, how they had withered when she had been in the hospital, even though Channah had watered them and pinched off the dead growth. Out of that forest, one rubber plant had remained, and when Saul could find no way to fit it in the car when they moved, Flo gave it to us: it survived for a week and then one night, while we slept, it had dropped all of its leaves on the living room rug.

"It smells so wonderful in there," my mother said when we left the shop.

I smiled and nodded, but what I really thought was that Daniel Rock had been right when he had told me his father's store smelled like a funeral parlor. The sweetness was so heavy it touched on rancidity, the lush fragrance spoiling even as you breathed it in. I had gone with my mother for Flo's sake, but also for my own: I had hoped Daniel would be there, but he was not.

"Is their boy still so brilliant?" my mother asked me. "That Daniel?"

That Daniel. "Brilliant as ever," I said, as if he were a flower whose dying had not yet begun.

That Daniel. Because we both had last names that began with *r* we had sat beside each other in most of our classes during all our years of school. Within the limits of that mandated proximity, affection prospered. If my pencil broke, Daniel gave me one of his. If one of us was ill, we called the other for homework assignments, and sometimes our conversations ventured beyond official information, touched with a joke or an expression of sympathy the realm of the intimate. As I approached puberty, Daniel was already in place, there beside me, the one on whom my fantasies would fix. That I was a shy and isolated girl and he was one of the best-liked boys in our grade heightened for me the wonder of our connection, however slight it might have appeared to others, and even the simplest exchange held for me the power of pledges and vows and prayers murmured to charitable gods.

While I'd steeped myself in stories of Europe—Flo's forsaken terrain so vivid to me I dreamed myself often a camp survivor, or one of those children who had lived for years like an animal in death-riddled woods—others my age were growing easily into their American lives. I pretended indifference to my classmates' aplomb, what seemed to me their breezy initiations into a culture I found as tricky and confusing as a foreigner might, and I learned the quiet contempt that blunts a bit the pain of exclusion. Daniel moved with as much grace over the cultural ground as I stumbled and lurched and retreated, yet I did not include him in my protective aloofness, I softened in his presence, I trusted him not to tease or snub me, and he rewarded my faith. I did not understand our kinship then, but I believed in it.

His parents were wealthy, their house a commanding Georgian in that section of the neighborhood where the monied clustered. But it was not affluence alone that distinguished him. Other boys, equally rich, lacked Daniel's perfect poise. At six and seven, when others fidgeted in their seats, he sat attentive as a yogi in meditative trance. He had an orator's mode of speech, as if he'd been taught enunciation, breathing, projection. At recess, he ran like an antelope, his body meshed with the currents of air that seemed to carry him over the blacktopped field. If he seemed an incarnation of the confidence privilege confers, there was nothing of the braggart about him—no swagger, no glibness, no condescending grin. He received his accolades modestly: swimming trophies, spelling bee championships, Science Fair medals, a starring role in *You Can't Take It with You*, valedictorian of the senior class, and letters of acceptance from Princeton and Yale.

That Daniel, is he still so brilliant?

2

In first grade he rescued me. We were hardly more than babies then, but each day's complexities were no less vexing than adult trials. In the cloakroom doorway, our teacher had hung a swing. At recess time, on rainy days, we could work on puzzles at our desks, or read, or take turns—twenty swings a child—on her improvised indoor playground. One day I'd stood in line for my chance to sail above the wooden floor, and halfway through my pendulum arcs, class bully Larry Cohen grabbed one of the ropes and jostled me to a stop.

"You're taking extras! You're on twenty-four!"

I would have broken into tears or slunk back to my desk, but Daniel Rock, who stood behind Larry in line, said quietly, "She has nine to go, Larry. Let her alone."

Larry Cohen paled. Who had ever stood up to him before? And in a voice so infused with compassion, so authoritatively generous, so forgiving even as it demanded justice that it seemed the voice—though its timbre was a child's—of a wise and aged man. I think it was that quality in Daniel's voice, even more than his action, that first bound me to him. I think I recognized something of my grandfather's voice in Daniel's. And Bishop Sheen's, on television, who preached his gentle sermons in just that tone. And President Eisenhower's, however true my parents' warning about him was: "A nice smile doesn't mean he cares about working people." When Ike talked, I believed he cared about me, or would if he knew me. I believed it about Daniel that day he saved me from Larry Cohen's mischief, and I believed it for the next eleven years, from grade to grade, our adjacent bodies as familiar to each other as a married couple who may not have very much in common, whose backgrounds may be drastically different, but who have found a way, nonetheless, to be comfortable together. Daniel and I lived two miles and worlds apart. My mother clerked in a department store to supplement my father's salary in the produce yards, and still we struggled. Mrs. Rock got her hair done once a week, her fingernails professionally polished, her face vacuumed and creamed and expertly made up. Mr. Rock worked half days much of the time, Rock's Florists "a little gold mine," as my mother said, and he spent leisurely afternoons playing poker at a private club downtown (often one of the players was a policeman in whose jurisdiction the club was located and on whose payroll he was included). When my father was washing his car on Sunday mornings, Mr. Rock was getting a full-body massage and a sauna and sometimes brunch at his father-in-law's palatial house. If Daniel and I had married—how often I dreamed it!—would such differences have been crucial? When would we have realized how foreign we were to each other, as if we had grown up in separate countries? Perhaps we would have reminded ourselves of the years we had sat side by side in school, as if preparing for a journey together, finding solace in one another's presence, enjoying those moments each day when we had rested in silence beside each other, knee grazing knee, or shoulders touching, as the seasons passed.

I never thanked Daniel that day he interceded on my behalf. Too shy, or embarrassed by my own rush of affection, I finished my swings and returned to my desk, offering Daniel only the briefest smile of gratitude. Even now, years after his death—he would kill himself hours after our high school graduation—in this long-considered story I am writing about him, I keep my eyes averted, I feel the press of his solitude, I alter enough of the facts to allow us both—narrator and subject—the final privacy fiction protects.

3

When I look at pictures of myself in my teenage years, I can see now the masklike smile, the glassy eyes, the mannequin rigidity in my posture. It was an ordeal then for me to walk across the room in view of others, and against their sight I steeled myself, held my breath, clenched my hands into weapons I pocketed, and forced myself into their midst. I bore secrets even I had forgotten—but I protected them fiercely from the scrutiny of others. My voice, still soft, was weaker then, thinned out, as if transmitted from a far distance, as if I resided somewhere other than in my body and radioed from that exile my almost-inaudible messages. "Can you speak up?" teachers asked, who did not understand the long journey each word had to make. "Chronic depression," a psychiatrist would name it years later, and perhaps that does explain my girlhood, clinically speaking, but a wiser healer would lead me past diagnosis to revelation: at five, like my great-grandmother Simca, I had given my spirit to grief, the loss of my grandfather buried in me like a dirge whose origins I could not remember but whose melody I heard when I woke and when I went to sleep, a lament clear as a solitary bird's whose call I came to learn, finally, was my own. I come from a long line of mourners: there is some solace in that.

I did not imagine having dates at all—longing seemed the form romance would take for me, forever—and I watched, with a kind of wistful resignation, the pairing from which I believed myself barred. In fact, before I graduated from high school I would have had two boyfriends, but both from other parts of the city, which afforded me a certain kind of safety. They would not know the degree to which I was excluded from the social life of my own school, and I would not have to suffer the judgments of my classmates about these boys who found my company desirable. I would be past thirty before I would understand the ways in which I still cut up my life into pieces of a puzzle no one, I hoped, would ever be able to assemble.

Phil Levine hated to read, laughed at the poems I wrote, brought along beer to the drive-in movies he took me to and kept his Camel cigarettes in his rolled-up shirt sleeve. I had met him at the zoo, where I often went in the summer, alone, taking two buses to Highland Park and wandering for hours among the captive animals. He sat down beside me on a bench in front of the seals and offered me some of his Sno-Cone. I was sixteen years old. He looked like a seedy Tab Hunter, his handsome disrepair suggestive to me of suffering and depth and missed opportunities in life. "He's a total stranger," my father said when I announced, in a voice so resolute I did not recognize it as my own, that I was going bowling with Phil Levine the following Saturday night. "My daughter doesn't go out with strangers." But who else would have asked me? Among the boys I knew, I was outside the circle of choice: they could not locate in my gestures or my tone the appropriate tribal signs. Among them for years, I remained a stranger, and if I went out at all, it would be with a stranger like myself.

When Phil graduated, he joined the Navy, and after that he wanted to run his father's bar. "He never was a boy for you," my mother would tell me when he stopped answering my letters. "You had nothing to talk to him about. Believe me, it's for the best. I was worried sick it would get more serious." I went to school with boys who knew they were going to college to become doctors or lawyers or professors in towns like Cambridge or Ann Arbor or Berkeley. In my neighborhood, becoming "professional men" in America completed the journey from Europe their grandparents or great-grandparents had begun, and the goals for which these boys strove fulfilled a mission of massive historical proportions of which we were all dimly aware. It was a boy like this I should have sought, my mother would remind me when Phil had gone, whose purposes I could understand, whose ambitions I could serve. But the only such boy I cared about was Daniel Rock, and beyond the range of my fantasies, I was sure he was out of reach, the world he lived in off limits to me, territory I would never inhabit. I had sent Phil letters at the base in Norfolk, Virginia: "I miss everything about you," I had lied, though I did miss necking with him in his Chevy sedan, undressing down to my underwear and letting him rub against me until the sticky wetness seeped through the nylon to the skin beneath—and all the time I would pretend it was Daniel Rock with whom I went "almost all the way" those strange Saturday nights of my junior year.

What was the line between "pretending" and "pretense"? That summer I met the son of a woman who worked downtown with my mother, and three, four, five times a week Eliot Roth drove from the distant suburb where he lived to my city block, then back again across town with me in tow, to the pizza place he liked, or the bowling alley near his house, or a party at the home of one of his friends. He was as respectful as Phil had proved flippant and dismissive, and he came "from nice people," my mother said, but I do not think I told Eliot one true thing all summer long. I invented for him a life I wished I had. I said I was the president of a sorority to which I did not even belong. I said I had just broken up with Daniel, imagining for myself years we had already dated, then the heartbreaking separation, and the possible reconciliation for which I yearned. "Would you go back with him?" Eliot said. I said I thought I would. "Well," Eliot said, "I guess I'll take my chances," and he looked so worried and rueful, I nearly began to believe in the romance I had conjured up. I created friends for Eliot I did not have—all of them off to summer camp, I said, or on vacations with their families—and played Scheherazade with anecdotes of slumber party pillow fights and shopping sprees and family intrigue of which I feigned knowledge, claimed to be the confidante of a dozen girls, thick since grade school, planning our futures together like sisters. As the summer came to an end, and school loomed, and I realized Eliot would surely learn how many of my stories were utter lies, I offered him the final fabrication: Daniel Rock wanted me back. In that duplicity, my truest dream triumphed. For a few days I lived in the fantasy's sweetness, and then school began. I was sure that the lies I had told Eliot all summer would be inscribed on the blackboards for everyone to read and mock, but the slates were clean and I was saved from the ridicule I feared.

We were seniors now. Two days before New Year's Eve, during our Christmas vacation, Daniel called me at home. I was in the kitchen helping my mother hang the café curtains she'd just washed and ironed, and I was on the stepladder, waiting for her to hand me a tier of flower-print chintz, when the phone rang.

"It's that Daniel," she said, holding out the receiver to me.

That Daniel. The room wavered. I held on to the window frame and stared for a moment into the branches of a snow-laden elm. The sun was milky today, pale, more like a moon, really, its light ghostly cold on the cold snow.

"Didn't you hear me?" my mother said. "You have a call."

Carefully I descended. Daniel had never phoned during a vacation before; we had no assignments this week between semesters, and schoolwork was the basis, the rationale, the catalyst for all our conversations. How many times had I abandoned that pretext, called him myself, lost my nerve and hung up as soon as anyone answered? How often had I wished that he would dial my house simply to talk or—more extravagant yet!—ask me to a movie or a dance or a dinner at Sodini's, where the college students went, where I knew Daniel took other girls for antipasto and garlic bread and pizzas with everything? Now it was happening—"I know it's last-minute," he said, "but I don't have any plans on New Year's Eve and I thought if you were free yourself, maybe we could do something together"—but instead of joy, sadness fell over me like a hood. I felt as if something we had forestalled all these years had finally overtaken us, snared us both, and we would have nothing to celebrate when 1961 slipped, irrevocably, into 1962.

"Oh, I'm free," I said, striving for buoyancy, and I gave him directions from his house to mine, the route I described mapped in my own body like blood-throbbing arteries my heart maintained.

"Isn't that nice?" my mother said when I hung up. I had forgotten she was even in the room—everything beyond the receiver in my hand had momentarily disappeared, as if that cold day's light had traveled from another world, entered our bare kitchen windows, and swallowed up in its vast nullity the fragile substance of our homely life. Slowly she came into focus, and I saw that her eyes were filled with tears, her cheeks pride-flushed, her hands lifted in preparation for applause or embrace: she had known, without my ever having told her, how long and painfully I'd hoped for Daniel's call and now she was paying me tribute, as if I had mastered the most difficult piano piece or solved a problem of terrible mathematical complexity.

Her hands dropped. "What's wrong?" she said. "I would think you'd be so happy."

Oh, how my melancholy injured and confused her. How hard my mother worked, all those years, to get me to "cheer up," "snap out of it," "look on the bright side of things for a change." Sometimes I thought she might break into a vaudeville routine, or a magic act, or a tumbling performance—anything to make me laugh, to release in me the flow of animation, as if it were a crucial bodily fluid dammed up in me, a knot of congested vitality she could somehow liberate. ("If your mother had been in the camps," Flo had said, "she would have saved lives.") Perhaps she saved mine, without my realizing it. Perhaps her efforts—which embarrassed me and angered me (wasn't I good enough for her as I was?)—soothed me, too. Not until I became a mother myself would I understand the helplessness she must have felt in the face of my loneliness, and the compassion, and the burden of guilt she bore.

"I don't know what's wrong." I sat down on a chair and cried. "I just don't know."

Every New Year's Eve my father bought a bottle of Mogen David Concord grape wine at the State Store, and my mother fixed a platter of chopped liver, flowered radishes, and mushrooms she had marinated in a spicy brine. She would bring out the cut-glass goblets that her mother had carried with her from Russia, and polish her sterling silver candlesticks, and iron her handmade lace bridge cloth that transformed the living room hope chest into a banquet table. Sometimes my father hung balloons from the ceiling light fixture, and sometimes he taped crepe paper streamers to the mantelpiece of the boarded-up fireplace. At nine, my mother would bring out the wine and the snacks, and my father would turn the television set to the channel carrying Guy Lombardo, live from Times Square. And then my parents would dance right along with the revelers in New York, and toast in the New Year, and sing "Auld Lang Syne" along with the televised crowd. "You feel like you're right there," my father would say. Television was still a miracle for him. "And you haven't even left your house." For years they urged me to join them, but I declined. "I'd rather read," I'd say, or "Oh, I think I'll go to bed early," or "Well, I have a poem I want to finish," and I would see them exchange a worried look, then one of them making a sign to the other to allow me my retreat, and my mother would say something like, "Then we'll wish you happy New Year early," and pour us all a tiny bit of wine and offer a toast to "our beautiful daughter, lots of good times in store for you." I can still hear the bell-like sound our glasses made, and I can taste that fruity wine, and I can remember lying alone in the dark, year after year, listening to the music and the laughter and then the chorus of strangers my parents joined, and I would add my voice to theirs. I would sing.

"You have a very nice voice," Daniel said, because it was minutes past twelve and we were listening to the Times Square celebration on the radio of his father's Buick, and I had just finished singing "Auld Lang Syne."

"Well, thanks," I said.

We had been to a movie downtown—Alec Guinness in *Tunes of Glory*—and then Daniel had driven us to the top of Mount Washington, the city's highest hill, from which we could see Pittsburgh spread out beneath us like a fallen sky, all those lights earthbound stars, and the steel mills' furnaces glowing like meteors spiraled in from space. At midnight, as if suddenly overrun by creatures we could not see in the dark, the croak of noisemakers surrounded us, and firecrackers exploded, and a panic of human cries rose up. We almost kissed—we leaned toward each other in that instinctual gesture—but then Daniel pulled back, tenderly, so that his retreat from me was a kind of caress, and I extended the distance between us, and when we were each pressed up against a car door, as far from each other as we could get in the car, the cacophony receded, and I started to sing, softly, that anthem to loss.

"Have you ever ridden the incline?" he said, looking out at the cable car stilled at the top of the steeply angled track.

"No," I said. I turned off the radio. The old year was gone. "Have you?"

He was looking straight ahead, through the window into that starry field below. "Sometimes I come out on a Saturday and ride it all day long."

"Maybe I'll come with you once," I said.

"Don't you want to know why I do it?"

"If you want to say."

"To get away from my parents," he said. "To get away from everyone."

"Well, I guess if I came along, you wouldn't be alone anymore."

"No."

I think at that moment we might have truly embraced—doesn't passion always depend on the admission of isolation and the desire to overcome it?—but suddenly it started to snow, heavily, the windshield blanketed in an instant, and Daniel said, "Well, I guess we better head home," and we drove down the winding snow-slicked roads in silence. We inched up the slippery front walk to my front door, and by the time we got there, his hair was covered with snow, he looked like an old man, that Daniel, as if the night had been decades long, a lifetime, and who could tell if he would ever see another New Year's Eve again?

4

A genealogy:

In the summer, say, of 1941, Jeannette Steiner married Gilbert Rock, her high school sweetheart, in the garden of her parents' Pittsburgh home. Judge Steiner conducted the ceremony himself, his rabbinical lineage apparent only in the cadences with which he delivered his part of the sectarian service. Throughout the garden, great ceramic urns brimmed with roses, carnations, and snapdragons. Silver bowls of roses bloomed like hothouse gardens in the center of each of the twenty linen-clothed tables arranged in a crescent under the huge tent, and above the head table a massive bower of blossoms arched over the bride and groom. Gilbert Rock's parents were florists and they had insisted on providing the flowers, even though the Steiners, wealthy from real estate and utilities stocks, could easily have financed every aspect of the elaborate wedding. The guests dined on salmon mousse, Chateaubriand, cherries flambé. They drank champagne and a vintage burgundy and coffee laced with rum. They sipped liqueurs from gold-plated cordials. They danced until morning to an orchestra partial to swing. As a social event, the affair was a great success, the Steiners and Rocks—all four of them children of turn-of-the-century immigrants—paradigms now of American opportunity come to fruition there under the rented tent.

In the next day's *Post-Gazette*, a photograph of the couple and a lengthy account of the wedding took up a third of the "Announcements" page. Jeannette, after all, was a judge's daughter, and status confers celebrity. Gilbert's family did not have the Steiners' credentials—college degrees, professional identity, country club manners— but they compensated with their flourishing business and

Mrs. Rock's twenty hours a week as a volunteer at Montefiore Hospital (she was on a first-name basis with a dozen doctors, and the hospital administrator himself attended the testimonial luncheon on her behalf).

Peau de soie, alençon lace, hand-beaded mother-of-pearl, satin-covered buttons: the paper described Jeannette's gown in ceremonial detail and noted also Gilbert's white tuxedo. The mothers of the bride and groom, the attendants, the flower girl and ring bearer: their costumes, too, fastidiously rendered by the reporter, who was, of course, covering a pageant, a masked ball, a small-scale mardi gras in which all the participants celebrate illusion, honor one another's disguises, raise their glasses to a dream. In the newspaper photograph of Gilbert and Jeannette, they wore those impermeable trancelike smiles that might otherwise alarm us, but which we deem appropriate for weddings, hypnotic rituals that they are.

Say Daniel's parents honeymooned in Cape Cod, renting for two weeks a house with water view, a private dock, a small sailboat they never used. Gilbert swam well, but Jeannette feared capsizing in the cold New England sea. She collected stones, which they would display in an oak curio cabinet they bought at an antiques fair and shipped back to Pittsburgh. They also bought a chess set with hand-carved ivory pieces, and Gilbert taught Jeannette to play. Each night in Cape Cod he defeated her, she feigned disappointment (chess did not interest her in the least, she would tell him years later; she hated the game), he solaced her, she feigned gratitude; and this ritual became foreplay for them, the chess giving way to arguments after the honeymoon but the strategies of their marriage firmly established in front of the fire on that chilly beach.

Or perhaps they did not go to Massachusetts at all. Perhaps they went to New York City, stayed in the honeymoon suite of the New Yorker hotel—a bucket of champagne and a box of chocolates on the bureau when they arrived, satin sheets on the canopied bed. A week of Broadway shows—Jeannette liked dramas, but Gilbert said, "Give me a musical comedy any day!"—and the Rockettes at Radio City Music Hall, and Lindy's cheesecake and Chinatown and the ferry ride to Staten Island. On top of the Empire State Building, Gilbert said, "Hey, let's ask that guy to take a picture of us together right by the rail, Jeannette," but she braked his enthusiasm: "I wouldn't look good, I'm too shaky," and he realized then that she was trembling and pale. "Did you get dizzy up there?" he asked her that evening, and she said, "Yes," but years later she would tell him, "You remember that day on the Empire State Building, how sick I was? You know why? Because for about two minutes up there, I wanted to jump off. I was on my honeymoon and I wanted to kill myself, Gilbert, that's the goddamned truth."

Before they bought the house in which Daniel would grow up, the Rocks lived in a pleasant apartment overlooking Schenley Park. On weekends they picnicked there, and often they walked the park's three-mile length to the city's huge botanical greenhouse, where exotic species in changing displays announced the seasons, commemorated holidays, honored the countries of famous dignitaries visiting the city from abroad. Gilbert studied the varieties of blooms, the combinations, the methods of arrangement. He was going after "big affairs"—bar mitzvahs, weddings, funerals, debutante balls—and he was looking for dramatic ideas. *Flowers with a Flourish* said the new sign over the door of Rock's Florists, the cards he sent to his growing mailing list, the ads he ran in the Pittsburgh papers. "Why can't we just enjoy ourselves?" Jeannette said, resenting the spiral notebook he carried with him on their excursions, the jottings he made at social functions they attended ("Try camellias on tiers," or "Hanging baskets of lobelia and baby's breath," or "Why not caladium, massed?"), the hours he spent poring through issues of *Horticulture* and *Better Homes and Gardens.*

In 1942, Gilbert Rock was drafted. Perhaps Jeannette had been pregnant with Daniel as my mother had been with me, or perhaps conception occurred during the week Jeannette spent with her husband in New Orleans, Louisiana, his overseas orders in the side pocket of his duffel bag. Against the terror of war, the Rocks' problems would have paled, and I can imagine the two of them staving off fear with romance, throwing themselves into a week of relentless courtship, marathon embrace, offering up to the gods their frenzied devotional rites. A fetus created out of such passion, however transitory, would have been charged with special energies, would have proceeded into the world as if on a star's trajectory.

What was your first memory? I am imagining a psychiatrist asking Daniel.

"Snow," he might have answered, not knowing he was recalling the seventh day of his life, Jeannette bearing him in her arms from the hospital entrance to her parents' car, the wind lifting the blanket folded over his face and his eyes startled open to the white swirls, his swaddled-warm skin stunned by the cold. That single blast could have signaled all the sorrow that the years ahead would bring him, wind-borne ice shards a fractured mirror in which the future danced. Our lives reveal themselves in such images, consigned to dreams as we age, but for an infant, they are the language his senses speak at birth.

"Snow," Daniel might have answered, the utterance releasing that first storm of primal prefigurations.

Jeannette decorated the nursery in the familiar pastels. The room seemed a shrine of animal icons—the duck-shaped lamp on the maple chest of drawers, the mobiles of felt birds and paper fish swimming in the air above the crib, to which decals of lambs had been affixed, the stuffed bears and the ceramic penguins and the tiny glass deer resting on the built-in bookshelves. Her mother-in-law had given Jeannette the rocking chair in which Gilbert had been nursed—"Sometimes I spent the whole night sitting up," Daniel's grandmother would say. "My Gilbert was such a fussy baby."

Daniel was not a fussy baby at all. "He could sleep through a war," Gilbert observed, not with pleasure. He had been discharged early after episodes of asthma, and his son's hours of undisturbable slumber felt like some sort of rebuke to the father, as if the child had already decided to live at a distance from the family, to create inside himself a retreat inaccessible to others, beyond the range of their scrutiny. Nights, Gilbert lay as poised for Daniel's wakings as did Jeannette, and when she slipped from their bed at their son's first whimper, Gilbert relaxed, the baby now returned to the parents' plane, those hours of impenetrable repose over, at least for a while.

As for Jeannette, she supposed she was grateful for the few demands that her child exacted, compared to the infants of her friends. Those women seemed always exhausted by their babies' difficulties—food allergies, colic, diaper rashes, colds and diarrhea and ear infections, parents and child awake for entire nights. Say Daniel suffered no such ailments. Say his constitution was more finely tuned than his peers', as if he had been born with an order of defenses other babies did not possess. His pediatrician pronounced him "a specimen of health," marveled at his reflexes, his coordination—"Very advanced," the doctor told Jeannette at Daniel's six-month visit. "He'll walk at nine or ten months. You probably have a future athlete on your hands."

"We must be doing something right," Gilbert said. Jeannette had just reported to him Dr. Paul's prediction. "Or maybe we got somebody else's kid in the hospital."

"That's not funny, Gilbert. That's not the least bit funny."

"I think it's funny."

"I don't," she said. "Don't ever make that sick joke again."

Did she know that Gilbert's "sick joke" disturbed her because it spoke to her own fear? Not that Daniel wasn't theirs—anyone could see his parents' features blended in his. What frightened Jeannette was the estrangement she felt from her own son, and that she sensed he felt from her. Even in the maternity ward, he had regarded her quizzically—Who are you? Who are you?—and months later she still did not feel that connection to Daniel her friends suggested they had with their infants: "As if we're one body," or "I can't remember my life before she was born." Jeannette could remember her life before Daniel quite well, and as for this experience of physical union, she guessed it had something to do with being highly sexed, which she wasn't, she just wasn't. "What's it like for you?" Gilbert had asked her once after intercourse, and she could tell from his expression that he was hoping for a graphic description of erotic pleasure, but Jeannette had answered, truthfully, "It's nice, it relaxes me," thinking of her father's weekly massages, her mother's pedicures.

Nursing Daniel, Jeannette felt a comfort on the same scale, but nothing of the intensity her friends expressed. When she weaned him, he switched easily to a bottle, his mother's breast relinquished without the slightest rebellion, and though she pretended gratitude for such an untroubled transition, secretly she envied the women with babies who shut their mouths to the rubber nipples, who clawed at their mothers' blouses, who wailed their rage at a loss of such elemental magnitude. Where was his need?

Thus, before he was a year old, Daniel Rock's parents had each decided that their uneasiness about their child was, in fact, his doing, a function of his nature, a problem no one else saw and which they never discussed with each other, but which announced itself, as if through a megaphone only the three of them could hear, every day of Daniel's life.

Perhaps Jeannette and Gilbert were right. Give them that. Perhaps Daniel would have been as private with any parents, his reserve encoded in his genes, his stoicism bone-bred, his character as fixed as his blood type.

What turns such neutral facts to grief?

The pediatrician was right: Daniel walked at ten months. From the start, he had a stride, purposeful and well-balanced, not the usual unsteady gait, the hesitant pace, the toppling over most babies suffer through until the ground feels familiar beneath their tiny feet. He understood gravity. He did not have to learn its unforgiving physics. His first steps looked practiced, the result of countless ascensions and falls, innumerable shufflings as if mastering a complex dance. In fact, he let go one day of the brocade sofa's welted edge and moved across the Persian rug as easily as Gilbert might, or Jeannette, as confident as any adult would be of the simple task. Playing still the parents of an ordinary boy, the Rocks cheered their son's accomplishment as if he'd traversed some forbidding terrain for the first time. He looked at them blankly, not understanding their excitement, confused by their applause. What were they celebrating? He had done nothing unusual. For seventeen years, his gifts would propel him beyond the power of conventional praise. From what source, then, does such a boy solicit verification? Against whose standards does he measure himself? His achievements magnified his loneliness, and though he pretended to be gratified by the honors bestowed upon him, in fact he was bewildered by a culture that deemed superior what for Daniel were ordinary efforts, easily won skills, simple luck. It was as if he stood already at the completion of his lifetime's efforts—famous in his field, perhaps; a national name—yet waiting still for a true vocation to announce itself, his spirit not yet summoned, or welcomed, into the world.

5

One morning at breakfast—her son off to school, the maid already arrived and doing the laundry—Jeannette Steiner Rock might have buttered a muffin and watched her husband scoop his soft-cooked egg out of its shell. The process was a delicate one, feminine almost, and Jeannette began to cry.

"Now what?" Gilbert said.

"I can't explain," she said.

She could, but she protected herself by pretending a kind of inchoate sadness. In fact, every time Jeannette Rock wept, she knew precisely the catalyst, and its larger context, and the particular need her tears revealed. In the past, she had allowed herself to be specific with Gilbert, to lay out her grievances in detail, to ask for precisely the kind of comfort she wanted at the moment. On such occasions, he had grown silent, then sullen, then worked toward some statement which rendered her supplication silly or selfish or even cruel—"You want me to get an ulcer, don't you? You want me to have a coronary, Jeannette"—so that she began to wonder if she weren't some sort of witch whose pain was a poisonous brew she stirred up and served to her husband, killing him dose by dose.

When she hated herself enough, she had an affair, two months of motel trysts with an orthodontist up the street. This was the summer Daniel was three. Jeannette had hired a sitter, explaining to Daniel that "Mommy's going to school for a while," explaining to Gilbert, "It's art appreciation. I need the stimulation." The sitter came three mornings a week at noon and stayed until five or so. Her name was Evelyn, and she was a black woman who took two streetcars from Homewood, where she lived with her husband, a laid-off steelworker, and five of their six children in a run-down rowhouse with bedrooms no bigger than Jeannette's walk-in closet. "All that house for the three of them," Evelyn would tell her family about the Rocks. "They could go for days and not even bump into each other. Rich and lonely. You can see it in the little one. Smart as a whip, that child is, but he's too good. You can tell a baby's hurting when he doesn't raise no fusses." He waited for her on the front steps, and he would hear her humming on the other side of the high privet hedge that hid the front yard from the street. Jeannette would be at the gilt-framed mirror over the foyer's marble-topped chest, checking her lipstick, applying another dab of rouge to her pink cheeks, making sure the seams on her stockings were straight. When she heard Evelyn's greeting—"How's my little sweet pea today?"—Jeannette came outside and though he remained seated, pushing his toy car in circles on the concrete stair, he waited anxiously for the final exchange—Jeannette's "Now you be good for Evelyn this afternoon," and Evelyn's "Say bye-bye to your mama, Daniel"—as if he knew how much each woman had to hide from the other in order to accomplish this transfer of power.

Evelyn took him for walks, named for him trees and flowers, taught him the calls of wrens, sparrows, robins, and crows. She explained the sky to him, how the next day's weather was embedded in the clouds he saw today.

"My daddy farmed," she told him. "That's how I learned so much nature. You city babies never even milked no cow." She sighed over his loss, and he felt his own sadness sprout. "I miss cows," he said, meaning it, though he had never seen any. Through Evelyn, he was having another life, and he came to dread Jeannette's return, her hand reclaiming him, leading him back into her distracted care.

One day she was late, or early—some departure from the schedule so that Evelyn and Daniel were not in the house, either because they were still walking or had gone out again. Either way, they were several blocks from the house when Daniel saw his mother stepping out of the orthodontist's light blue coupe, walking around to the driver's side, and kissing this man quickly, quickly on the mouth. "Oh my lord!" he heard Evelyn gasp, though as if from a far distance, while his mother, fifty yards away, was visible to him in more detail than ever before, so that it seemed to him he could see the pores of her skin, the small mole on her neck, the ridges on her polished fingernails. His eyes burned, as if the sight at which he stared were dangerously, injuriously, bright. Evelyn spun him around and took him home and sang a healing hymn until Jeannette arrived. In mid-August, she ended the affair and Evelyn stopped coming. Daniel mourned for her for months, but Jeannette Rock had no sign of her son's grief. In his first months, he had learned to hide his unhappiness from her, as if it were his wounded twin of whose birth Jeannette was somehow ignorant, an unfortunate infant Daniel knew she would deny, were she ever to learn he existed.

For a while she saw a psychiatrist at a time when one kept that measure quiet, and then she got pregnant—Daniel was in school by now, so Jeannette decided she could manage another, with help—and lost the baby at four months, and grieved for the infant girl she named, to herself, Claire. Home from the hospital, she stayed in bed for weeks. Daniel carried trays to her room. He made her get-well cards. He brought compresses for her headaches and her weepy red eyes. "You take such good care of me," she told him. "You are the best boy."

What about Gilbert? During those years, he consoled his wife exactly to the point at which she allowed herself to yield to his solace, at which moment he withdrew, leaving her, as she saw it, more wounded than she had been—or had sensed herself to be—before his fleeting ministrations. For his part, Gilbert said, "I'm telling you, Jeannette, you are sucking me dry." Finally, she arrived at a numbness her mother noted as "maturity" ("I have always thought Jeannette lacked a certain degree of maturity" is how she might have put it). Judge Steiner—who had never liked his son-in-law, preferring for his daughter a man more cerebral, a man of finesse, a man exactly like himself, he might have put it, had he ever stated aloud to anyone his dissatisfaction with Gilbert—told Jeannette, "Well, I'm glad to see you finally content with your choices. You have a certain peace about you now, and it becomes you." Gilbert, too, decided that Jeannette had finally "settled down," blamed all the troubles of the prior years on "hormones," and took up golf in celebration of the apparent state of normalcy into which his marriage had drifted.

Only Daniel recognized his mother's continuing misery. I imagine she invited him into it, as if into a secret room that only the two of them visited. Something clandestine suggested itself in the look of pain she fixed on him alone. This is for you, the look suggested, as seductive as a sexual message might be. Was this what people meant when they talked about a parent and a child "being close"? He could never be sure if he should feel honored that she spared him from her sham, or horrified that she let the others believe she was "fine, just fine" while he had to bear the truth alone.

*   *   *

The first time I saw Jeannette Rock, she came to Colston Elementary School for the fourth grade's Mother's Day Concert. In 1954, few women worked and it was customary to schedule during the day school events to which mothers were invited. Thirty folding chairs were set up in the Cafeteria-cum-auditorium where we would perform, and Jeannette sat in the front row. She wore a name tag that said *Hello, I'm Mrs. Rock.* She wore a little pillbox hat with a veil that looked like a shadow fallen across her brow. She wore a shimmering taffeta shirtwaist that rustled when she moved, and high heels exactly the same maroon as her dress, and a pearl choker and white gloves my mother might have sold her on one of her many shopping expeditions downtown. On the counter behind which my mother worked, Jeannette might have set her elbow and held her hand aloft, the professionally manicured fingers splayed, the wrist locked. My mother would have stooped down to retrieve from the drawers behind her the three pairs of gloves Jeannette had chosen from those on display. Rising with the appropriate boxes, my mother would have taken out the first right-hand glove and begun the process, so hard on her own hands, of pulling and smoothing and pulling again the cloth or the kid leather down each of Jeannette's fingers and then taut over her palm and the back of her upraised, expectant hand. Later, my mother would have seen Jeannette's name on her Charge-a-plate. "Oh, you're the florist, my daughter and your son are in the same class." And Jeannette would have looked at my mother warily, my mother mistaking the expression for disdain—"Women like that, they think they're the Queen of Sheba"—but actually Jeannette Rock would have been threatened by anyone who reminded her that Daniel had his own life apart from her, friends in whom he might confide, the parents of these friends, teachers—all of them learning from him the secrets about his mother she did

121

not even know she had entrusted to him. Did she sit in the front row on the morning of the fourth grade's Mother's Day Concert because she wanted the very best seat, or was she placing herself between her son and the world, fixing on him, even as he sang solo "When Irish Eyes Are Smiling," her suffering stare?

6

By the time Daniel was five years old, the elder Rocks had retired from the business and left Rock's Florists, grossing two hundred thousand a year, to Gilbert. He employed two full-time clerks, two part-timers, three arrangers, a janitor, and three drivers for his delivery vans. On Saturday mornings, he went in "to do the books," and he took Daniel with him, the father and son walking like the synagogue-bound the eight blocks from their treed residential enclave to the shop. Half the stores on Murray Avenue shut down on Saturdays, their owners observant Jews whose lives were still governed by the commandments of the faith. Sometimes Daniel pretended that he and his father were going to Sabbath services, the week of secular enterprise set aside for a day of contemplation. He wished his father would wrap them each in prayer shawls, place a yarmulke on each of their heads, lead Daniel into the high-ceilinged sanctuary to a wooden pew close to the rabbi's podium, the sacred ark that housed the Torah, an ornately carved backdrop before which the rabbi swayed. Through the stained-glass windows, the softened light would come in like honey and blue water and dew-dappled grass. Cities would fall away in that transforming wash; commerce would die; the business of the world would sputter and fail and the mysteries would gather like flocks of birds in the windows of deserted stores and schools and the cars abandoned on the silent roads. Out of that quiet, the men's voices would rise in mimetic chant, songs of the firmament filling the metamorphosed hall.

"You'd think they'd never left Europe," Gilbert said.

He and Daniel were walking to the store. A group of Chasidim, chattering in Yiddish, had just swept past them into the yeshiva, the tails of their long black coats lifting like crows' wings, their earlocks' feathers fluttering under their broad-brimmed hats.

"I like them," Daniel said, wishing he could follow them inside.

"They're in America," Gilbert said, dropping his son's hand. "They should act like Americans."

Two blocks more and they were at the shop. Gilbert Rock, American, had just taken off the padlock from the front door—the help wouldn't be in for another hour—when Manny Cohen hailed him from his pumps across the street. He was not just saying hello. He was agitated, his arm flailing like a scythe, but his words were garbled by the noise of passing cars. Inside, the phone was ringing. "Ah, let it go," Gilbert said, not to Daniel, whose presence the father seemed to have dismissed a moment after their disagreement. Knowing himself invisible—because that was the status Gilbert's fallen face conferred on the boy whenever Daniel's notions countered Gilbert's own—Daniel followed his father to the station like an agent trailing an unsuspecting subject.

"What's the matter?" Gilbert said to Manny. "Is Fay sick?"

Manny Cohen ran his grime-stained hands through his thinning hair, streaks of oil tracked across his forehead. "Fay? What in the hell would Fay have to do with—"

"She just had her surgery. I thought—"

"The wife is fine, Gil." He was bouncing on the balls of his feet, the news he had to tell a tic invading his limbs.

"So what is it then? Were you held up?"

Daniel stood behind the premium pump that Manny and his father faced. Manny had not seemed aware of the boy at all. Had the station owner's distress subsumed all other observations, or had Gilbert truly caused his son to vanish from the scene? All children are spies. Many relish the role. Others, like Daniel, resist the subterfuge into which they feel forced. Hidden, Daniel wanted to reveal himself; silenced, he wanted to insist that the men recognize him as witness to their talk. But the odor of gasoline was so strong it seemed to thicken the air around him, clogging his throat so that he could not speak.

"I'll show you," Manny said. He took Gilbert by the arm and steered him to his vans. Daniel followed the men through the viscous element, his breathing labored, his movement difficult. Did he want to run away because they were ignoring him or assumed he was not there, or did he glean already the news he would not want to know?

His father took in the damage calmly: shattered windshields, slashed tires, black paint streaked like ribbons across the bodies of the trucks.

"Shit," said Manny. "You're not even surprised, are you?"

Gilbert looked away.

"Look, Gil," Manny said. "I'm sorry if you're in some kind of trouble or something, but I'm clean over here, you know what I mean? I don't have any connections with those hoods, they leave me alone, and I want those fucking trucks out of here right now, you can't use my tow truck neither, I got to protect myself, I—"

The angrier he grew, the raspier his voice became, until he was entirely hoarse and no sounds came out of his mouth at all.

"I play cards with the bastard," Gilbert said. "I thought he was a friend of mine."

Manny raised a finger to his lips. With his other hand, he gestured to Daniel standing in a pile of glass shards, at risk, perhaps already injured, every word Gilbert uttered jeopardizing further his son's well-being.

"Go back to the store!" Gilbert barked. "Right now!"

He left his father with the wrecked vans and raced through the grounds of the smelly station across the street to the flower-filled shop, its perfume now rancid to him, spoiled. He thought he would be sick. Stumbling toward the bathroom, he knocked a terrarium from a table in the back room where the arrangers worked, and the dirt spilled across the wooden floor, uprooted plants strewn like tiny trees torn from the earth by some violent squall.

If Manny was "clean," then Gilbert was "dirty," sullied by "trouble," "connections with those hoods," "those fucking trucks." And who was the card-playing "bastard" on whose friendship Gilbert had thought to rely? Daniel tried to vomit up the words he had heard, but they had entered his memory, they were history now, and it would take more than one purgation to vanquish that nausea, if an antidote existed at all. Behind his placid exterior, would his innards tremble, the queasiness a chronic affliction for which he would find no cure, though no doctor ever discovered the symptoms about which Daniel never complained? ("A specimen of health," the pediatrician had said, and Daniel Rock never countered that appraisal.)

Later he would learn that "the bastard" was Frank Zatelli, a Pittsburgh mobster in the Teamsters hierarchy; when lower-echelon organizers had visited Gilbert in the shop and suggested to him, quietly, in the small rear room he used as his office, that union men should drive his delivery trucks, he had explained to them that none of his drivers worked full-time, that his was a family business. Union wages to part-timers in a family business would be "fiscally irresponsible," he'd said, "not good business at all."

"You having all your trucks smashed up wouldn't be good business neither, Mr. Rock," one of the organizers had said.

Gilbert had mentioned this conversation to Frank Zatelli at poker that Wednesday. Frank had given Gilbert one of his many smiles—he responded to all comments and questions with smiles, different ones suggesting different responses, though this decoding was up to the receiver, Frank preferring the enigmatic stance.

"You'll talk to them, Frank, right?"

Another smile, which Gilbert had guessed to be assurance.

Gilbert had guessed wrong.

"Just forget what you heard," Gilbert told Daniel. The boy was making a house of Styrofoam blocks the arrangers used for anchoring flowers in a bowl. "You're too young to understand these things. And don't worry about the trucks. That's what insurance is, it takes care of everything."

The house fell, the blocks landing silently at Daniel's feet. Who would know anything at all had collapsed, unless they were staring right at it?

"I'll have it for you Tuesday, Frank," he would hear his father on the kitchen phone. "And Frank, leave Cohen alone, he's an old man."

Or his parents arguing on the wicker-furnished sun porch: "I want to ask my father for advice, Gilbert. We need legal advice."

"You breathe a word of this to the judge, Jeannette, and you might as well put me in jail yourself. And who the hell are you to tell me how to run a business? Who earns the living here?"

Quietly, quietly, Daniel Rock would climb the stairs, go to his room, lie down on his bed. Closing his eyes, he would remember the Styrofoam house, the way it had broken to pieces without a sound, and how, if he hadn't been looking at it just then, he would not have known it had collapsed at all.

In my parents' conversations, references to mobsters at work in our neighborhood surfaced like occasional shark fins yards from shore—I recognized the danger, I shuddered, the fin sank, I forgot the sighting.

A new supermarket on Murray Avenue, my mother said, was "Mafia." She and my father exchanged a name. "His mother would drop dead a second time," my father said. My mother sighed, perhaps taking the dead mother's place, grieving on her behalf for this son, the crook.

A local home improvement company—shingles, siding, storm windows and doors—promised customers financing, sent them to loan companies everybody knew to be "the Mob." My father said, "You know what they do to you if you miss a payment? They bust your nose."

Rock's Florists were "tied in," my mother said. I was doing my homework at the kitchen table and my parents believed that when I studied, I was in a state not unlike sleep, unaware of their exchanges, out of hearing range.

"No kidding," my father said. "That I didn't know."

Tied in. I imagined Mr. Rock at the end of a long tether, the Untouchables' Eliot Ness reeling in the florist like a fish. "Do you have proof?" I said, lifting my head from my French book. "Because if you don't I think it's wrong to say a thing like that."

"Where did she come from?" my father asked.

My mother shrugged.

"So do you?" I said. "Yes or no."

My mother said, "You hear things, that's all I can tell you. You hear things."

"That isn't good enough," I said then, as if I, too, had been slandered.

Years later, a maker of stories myself, I understand what my mother meant. Where do they come from—gossip, dream, memory, fiction? You hear things, that's all I can tell you. You hear things.

7

"You're going to hear things about me," his grandfather was saying, "and since you're my family, I want you to hear my version first."

They had just finished dinner in the Steiners' formal dining room: a three-tiered crystal chandelier the judge and his wife had brought back from a trip to Venice; Louis XIV table, twelve chairs, a china-filled breakfront, and a matching mahogany sideboard on which rested the mirrored tray holding the decanters of liqueur, the delicate cordial cups. The judge was pouring the adults amaretto, root beer for his grandson.

"You're excused now," Jeannette said to Daniel.

"Not at all," Judge Steiner said. "I want him to stay."

"Well, I don't," Jeannette said. She was close to tears. "Gilbert?"

Mrs. Steiner said, "Defer to your father, dear. You are in his house." She was a diminutive woman, her hands so tiny that the diamond-and-emerald cocktail ring in its antique gold setting looked strange, as if she were a child costumed as an adult, her sleek silver bun a wig she could remove, revealing a head of girlish auburn curls.

"Well, what is this about, Dad?" Gilbert asked his father-in-law, although the younger man already knew. The rumors were traveling through the neighborhood like a password one person whispered to another, a secret nobody wanted to keep.

"I've been subpoenaed by the House Un-American Activities Committee," Judge Steiner said. "I have nothing to hide." His hand was trembling and the liqueur he was holding spilled on the tablecloth. "I have nothing to be ashamed of."

"Dad, please—" Jeannette was pulling Daniel from his chair now. He was ten years old and this was October 1954. He knew what "subpoenaed" meant; his grandfather was a judge, after all, and Daniel had been hearing legal language all his life. He knew who McCarthy was, and his committee—the hearings were televised, the paper's front page a constant advertisement. He knew about hiding, and shame—his mother and the man in the pale blue car, his father and Frank Zatelli ("You breathe a word of this to the judge, Jeannette," Gilbert had said, "and you might as well put me in jail yourself"). Why was his grandfather shaking?

Gilbert said, "Just don't be noble down there. That's my only advice, if you don't think I'm out of line, Dad."

"I can hear," Daniel reassured his mother, in a tone so grave a person more attuned to the boy would have understood the message those words conveyed: *I have been hearing bad news all my life.*

Or Judge Steiner might never have said a word to his family.

In the den, they were watching a Pirates game. Gilbert said, "Hey, Danny, get me a glass of ginger ale, will you, not too much ice?"—and as soon as she believed her son was out of hearing range, Jeannette would offer, like a bulletin breaking into regular programming, "My father's been subpoenaed, Gilbert."

"Who by?" He would spring to his feet, as if an adversary had just burst into the room. "A grand jury?" Thinking of Zatelli.

She looked away from her husband, his color-drained face.

"The House Un-American Activities Committee," she said.

Gilbert Rock whistled.

Daniel listened from the hallway. All children are spies.

"Just so he doesn't decide to be noble," Gilbert said, back in his chair, lighting a cigar. "Just so he looks out for his own hide."

History, I used to think, belonged to Europeans—all that terror and turbulence from which my grandfather had fled, which Flo had survived like one of the feathers that flies free from the slaughtered bird. In America, though I knew about the Ku Klux Klan and the Mafia and a place called Korea where the Laskers' boy died, still I believed that one of the guarantees of citizenship—was it written in the Bill of Rights?—was a life apart from History. My parents might talk politics from time to time. We watched the McCarthy hearings on television—my father maintaining a running critique of "the momser," my mother more distressed that Roy Cohn, "a nice Jewish boy like that," should be McCarthy's devoted counsel—but how did that spectacle impinge on our lives? How different was it, really, this public purge, from the other shows we watched together, my mother bringing out a steady supply of snacks—a bowl of fruit, cookies on a plate, a bag of potato chips she warned us "makes a mess if you're not careful."

If my family existed in such unworldly innocence, I

imagined for the Rocks an even more protected world, affluence invoking a pristine order in their daily lives, conferring grace, Daniel's poise a reflection, I believed, of a household where thoughts and actions were as polished as the furniture and floors, as safe from upheaval as the jewelry women like Jeannette kept in locked leather boxes on their bedroom dressers.

So Gilbert Rock might be "tied in" to mobsters. So Judge Steiner was subpoenaed by the House Un-American Activities Committee and questioned for five hours about a certain rally he had attended in New York City in 1939, about certain meetings organized by colleagues at the University of Pittsburgh, where, at the time, he was teaching a course in constitutional law. So he informed on his friends. So he offered up names. So he was hospitalized for several months later that year "for extreme exhaustion," the newspaper articles said, accounting for his early retirement from the Court of Common Pleas. What had any of that to do with the beautiful Georgian house on the professionally landscaped lot? I swept the image clean, as if I were the Rocks' caretaker clearing the front walk of debris a storm scattered there during the night.

8

In the sixth grade, we had a male teacher, and in 1955 such a presence in an elementary school classroom aroused the most profound curiosity. I am speaking of a time in which the things that men and women did and did not do was as clearly codified as the regulations governing automobiles: drive on the right side of the road, stop on red, always turn the headlights on at night. We might as well have written into law the rules of gender, and the penalties for breaking them.

He was a slight man, and fair, and his eyes were a milky blue. At times he looked transparent (not frail), as if light passed through him, as if he were a filter of some sort. When he stood in front of a window, it would not have been surprising if all his bones had become visible. His voice approached song. I mean the tenor's pitch of his speech, the honied element out of which his words were formed.

"A moment of quiet now."

He said that every morning, after the Pledge of Allegiance and the principal's psalm-reading piped into each room. We would close our eyes and sink into stillness and wait for Mr. Matthews' summons back into activity. Once I peeked, raising my lids the slightest fraction. We looked like children at a seance, our teacher guiding us into another realm. He sat behind his desk, his palms turned up, as if to catch rain. His face was so still it seemed to be made of alabaster, and the even breaths he drew reminded me more of the sea than a man's breathing. I turned in my seat to look at Daniel. He was a perfect replica of Mr. Matthews' repose, he and the teacher altered in a way the rest of us were not, as if Daniel had mastered long ago the state of detachment in which the rest of us were novices.

We began penmanship that year. Each of our desks was equipped with an inkwell, and Mr. Matthews distributed pens the second week of class. I went to Woolworth's and bought my bottle of dark blue ink, a box of extra nibs. That purchase had for me the same power as buying my first bra or pack of cigarettes or, years later, a car in my own name. To write in script! Mr. Matthews was guiding us out of self-conscious, subliterate block-print consciousness into a higher plane of being, where thought, I sensed, would turn fluid and graceful as the lined letters we drew on the page. Language became a dance to me then, my hand gliding like an ice skater over the lined paper, my movements all swirls and dips and curves and flourishes.

One day we came to school and a substitute greeted us. She was a middle-aged woman with a cap of brown curls and she looked oddly out of place behind the desk I'd been shocked to see a man occupy in September. "Your teacher will be absent for a week," she told us. "A member of his family has passed away."

She gave us a moment to absorb the grave truth that teachers have lives as littered with pain as anyone else's. "Take out your spellers," she said. Slowly we lifted our desk tops, the wood grown heavier or the air suddenly thickened, so that it seemed an effort to complete the routine task.

Daniel raised his hand.

"Young man?"

"We should do something for him."

"Do?"

"We should write him sympathy notes," Daniel said, sounding like a kindly instructor, speaking not too differently from Mr. Matthews himself.

"Well," she said, "we have so much to cover."

"We could do it for penmanship," Daniel said. "That comes right before lunch."

"That's a good solution," she said, flustered, as if a problem had ever existed.

How canny of Daniel to have invented a compromise that took into account her bureaucratic devotion to rules. So much to cover. As if we were tarring a road or laying sod on a vacant lot.

Daniel's hand was still in the air.

"Yes?" she said.

"May I go to the principal's office and get his address? Or maybe the secretary will mail the letters for us."

"All right," she said. She wrote him a hall pass. She smiled at him brightly, and then at the rest of us, but it was clear she was nonplussed by this boy, his generous nature, his industry on its behalf. Who are you, she might have been wondering, and who is this Mr. Matthews?

("And who is this Mr. Matthews?" my father had said at supper, after the first day of school. "It's not a man's job, teaching babies."

"It's very nice," my mother had said. "You don't expect it. But I think it's very nice."

"He's from Albuquerque, New Mexico," I'd said, as if that explained his odd choice of professions.

"They probably have a shortage there," my father had said. "Of women."

"Sure," my mother had said. "It makes sense."

It did not make sense at all, but I knew I was not to question the logic of such a deduction. What my parents needed were explanations, real or invented, for deviations from the norm. In the fifties, the norm had such power over people's imaginations that you might have thought it a physical entity, like the pyramids, or the great brooding rocks at Stonehenge. All mystery disappeared into the norm—imagine a mouth or a cavernous doorway from which emitted a constant and undifferentiated static to which we grew accustomed. Only troublemakers named it noise.)

We penned our notes to Edward Matthews—the substitute wrote the words "sympathy" and "condolences" and "bereavement" on the board—and Daniel moved from row to row, collecting our papers as if he had become the teacher, as if he, not the brown-haired woman, were Mr.

134

Matthews' true replacement. He put them all into a manila envelope the secretary had given him, on which she'd already written Mr. Matthews' Albuquerque address. At lunchtime, Daniel delivered our offerings to the office, and even Larry Mintzer, who loved to make fun of all magnanimity, held his tongue this time.

Often Daniel stayed after school to help Mr. Matthews clean the room or change the bulletin board display. How many mornings did I arrive to find Daniel already there, boy and man engrossed in some early-hours conversation, some private exchange? Between the two a certain rapport developed, nourished by their mutual curiosities, their common sympathies, and—I would realize later, looking back—the loneliness each recognized in the other and sought to salve.

Did they have other encounters, outside the classroom? Did they meet for milk shakes in the soda fountain across the street from school? Did they go together to the museum in Oakland where the great dinosaur replicas loomed? Did Mr. Matthews take Daniel to Buehl Planetarium, the domed ceiling in the darkened amphitheater transformed into a glittering sky of infinite depth?

Probably not. Jeannette would not have countenanced her son's spending that much time with a man more fatherly than Gilbert knew how to be, more nurturing than Jeannette herself. But I can allow student and teacher the friendship that would have fed them both. The closed palm of the past opens and a hundred seeds scatter, each one a story that grows like a tree, deeply rooted and aspiring and essentially true.

Once upon a time, then, Daniel took the streetcar to Mr. Matthews' apartment in Shadyside, a neighborhood of students and professors and artists prospering and not. "Too

135

many beatniks," my mother would say when we browsed in the Walnut Street boutiques and galleries and specialty food shops. "And too much of that." She would gesture toward a couple kissing on the sidewalk. I liked the easy tolerance that governed the place, the willingness there to set aside "standards," many of which I secretly chafed at, though I was not old enough yet to rebel.

Once upon a time Daniel walked up the three flights of the converted mansion to apartment 302 and knocked on the solid oak door. Inside, classical music—Dvořák's *New World Symphony*—played, and Daniel knocked again, to make sure he would be heard over the orchestral crescendos.

"Hello, Daniel!" Mr. Matthews sang, sounding like an instrument himself.

He was just coming up the steps Daniel had mounted, the teacher's arms laden with grocery bags.

"I ran out to get some things for lunch," he said, breathless. "I thought I'd get here before you."

"I hear music in there," Daniel said.

"I leave it on for Chester."

"Who's Chester?" Daniel was unlocking the door with the key Mr. Matthews had retrieved with his free hand from the pocket of his poplin jacket.

"My cat," the teacher said. "He's very fond of recordings."

Inside, the gray Persian posed on the high curved back of the sofa. Heavy blue drapes were pulled back to let daylight fill the seven-foot-long windows. Bookcases reached to the ceiling, their shelves jammed with books in bright jackets.

"Have you read all these?" Daniel asked.

"Oh, yes, I'm something of a writer myself. Short stories. When you're older, I'll let you read some of them," Edward Matthews said.

There. The projection into a future in which their kinship continued to flourish. A legacy proffered by the man to the boy.

That afternoon they played Parcheesi at a cherry dropleaf table. Mr. Matthews had made them lunch—chicken sandwiches and cole slaw and ice-cream roll for dessert.

"I have thoroughly enjoyed your visit," he said as Daniel left.

They shook hands.

"I enjoyed it too," Daniel said. "I hope you'll invite me again."

But he would not be invited again. Jeannette would have explained to him that "Mr. Matthews doesn't have children of his own, you see, and he tends to get too . . . close . . . to little boys," the disgust she had stirred up in herself bleeding through the pleasant tone she had decided to adopt, so that her words, if visible, would have looked like curdled milk.

"I don't know what you mean," Daniel would have protested, knowing something final had been decided for him, some small piece of his fate set into irrevocable place.

"Of course not," Jeannette would have said, nearly believing now her own fabrication. "You're just a child."

Would she have started the rumors about Mr. Matthews' "tendencies," or would she have responded to gossip already rife? Either way, Daniel would not have been invited to his teacher's home again, and Edward Matthews would move on to another school after a single year at Colston.

"I hear he moved to New York," someone told Jeannette at the beauty parlor where she went every Thursday afternoon for a wash and set, and a cut every third week.

"It's certainly no loss to us," she might have said, turning down the dryer a notch. "He never should have been hired at all."

9

"What I heard," my mother would tell me the summer Daniel killed himself, "was he met a girl in Cape Cod and she broke his heart." She paused, as if considering the words she had spoken, looking them over as if they were items in a store she might or might not buy. "It happens. You hear it so much—a broken heart— you think it's baloney, but actually, it does happen. A terrible, terrible thing."

Say her name was Caroline Bell. Say she wore her long black hair in a single braid down her back or twisted atop her head. Although her eyes were small, deep-set, their light color lent them drama against her olive skin. Gold-flecked hazel eyes, like fish glinting in a dark sea.

They liked to meet in the early morning, before the adults rose, and comb the beach together for shells and stones and the occasional man-made relic delivered by the tide. Once they found an algae-crusted pocket mirror, the glass intact, the filigreed frame like the delicate bones of a fossilized bird. Daniel spent the day picking the mirror clean, and then he polished it and wrapped it in a silk scarf he bought at a boutique in town.

Say he was staying at his grandparents' summer house on Nantucket. The Steiners and the Bells were friends; Caroline's father was a lawyer in Boston, and he and the judge had met years ago at the Bar Association's convention in New Orleans. On Caroline's birthday, the Bells invited the Steiners for dinner—poached salmon and a hot potato salad Mrs. Bell was famous for.

"Happy birthday," Daniel said. He gave Caroline her gift. She had already opened her presents from her family, and the sampler of French perfumes from the judge and his wife—Jeannette and Gilbert would not arrive in Nantucket for another week.

"Oh!" she said, recognizing the restored mirror. "The buried treasure!"

She turned the piece around in her hand and the glass sent spires of reflected light across the ceiling and wall. Later, she would kiss him, after the adults had taken her ten-year-old brother into town for an ice-cream cone. Later, she would let him unbutton her blouse and kiss her small white breasts. Later, she would let him stroke her lace-edged panties and then, hidden between two dunes far down the beach, he would take off his tennis shorts and cotton briefs and she would let him come on her belly's flushed skin.

"So you're seeing a lot of this Caroline Bell," Gilbert said, his second morning there.

He and Daniel were sitting on the porch overlooking the water. Gilbert was eating half a grapefruit with a serrated spoon.

"I see her every day," Daniel said. He had finished his cornflakes; beginning to rise, he pushed back from the wrought-iron table.

Gilbert reached out and put a hand on his son's knee.

"Well, let's talk about this, Danny. Man-to-man, know what I mean?"

Jeannette had forced him to do this. "He's obsessed" was how she'd put it.

"He's on vacation," Gilbert had said, as if that were an equivalent emotional condition.

Finally he'd agreed to "find out what's going on."

"I don't care what you do," he said to Daniel, "so long as you don't knock her up."

Which he did not.

*   *   *

139

"She didn't write him after the summer," my mother said. "At least that's what I heard."

Caroline Bell didn't write. Daniel wrote, sometimes two letters a day, then one, then a letter a week. Once he called her in Boston. She lived in Cambridge, not far from Harvard Yard, and she rode her bike to a private day school overlooking the Charles River. The maid told him she wasn't home. The maid said she had no idea when Caroline would return, but she would certainly tell her that Daniel Rock had called from Pittsburgh, she certainly would tell her that. Caroline did not call him back, and she never answered a single letter he sent. In his last note to her, he wrote, *Don't feel guilty. I enjoyed knowing you. I wish you all the best in your future.* He signed it, *Love, Daniel.*

I do not believe a single loss shatters any heart. All pathology reports confirm the history of harm the cells carry from birth, and if hope were an organ, we could examine its own slow death.

("Snow," he might have said. "The first thing I remember is snow.")

On the day we graduated from high school, it rained. My parents took pictures of me in my robe, in front of our house and on the wide steps of Soldiers and Sailors Hall. I am a blur, the image of time receding even at the moment of its capture on film.

"Who can believe you're going to college in a few months?" my mother said. She turned up her palms as if the drizzle they caught could help her understand how it was that I had grown up so quickly, eighteen years gone like the sunshine, overnight, gloom and celebration mingled now this dreary commencement day.

The Rocks probably took an album's worth of photographs, and movies as well. Gilbert might have tape-recorded the ceremony, especially Daniel's valedictory speech, a gloss on Henry David Thoreau's notion of simplicity and how we needed to strip the clutter from our lives and minds. Perhaps if I called up the Rocks today, they would take down the album from the shelf in the hall closet, and Gilbert would bring up the projector from what we called in that time a "rumpus room," the paneled basement space complete with bar and hi-fi and a tropical fish tank built into the wall.

"A boy who had everything," my mother said. "How could he throw it all away?"

Four A.M., graduation morning. Outside Daniel's bedroom, the downspout breaks away from the gutter and a rush of water buffets the window glass. The sound wakes him. Perhaps he gets out of bed and raises the shade. In the early light, the backyard shimmies. Columns of boxwood, the alyssum-bordered patio, the garden's grid of brick paths demarcating dense rectangular plantings of salvia and pansies and glowing marigolds, the line of evergreens along the chain-link fence, the two towering maples between which the mesh hammock swings—all a watery swirl through the sudden flood.

I imagine him putting on his terry-cloth robe and his corduroy slippers. He walks down the stairs, through the kitchen, the mud room, and out into the yard. He feels his feet sinking into the sod. He lies down on the drenched hammock and lets the rain pelt him there. He watches the edges of the house fuzz, the roof slip off center, the mortar between the bricks soften. It is like seeing his life itself waver and dissolve. Inside, his parents sleep, oblivious in their dry bed. Later, he will join them in the kitchen for blueberry waffles, "because it was his favorite," Jeannette would remember later. "At least he had his favorite breakfast." She will tell him that morning, "I think you should wear your glen plaid suit today. Gilbert, don't you think he should wear his glen plaid?" Gilbert will shrug. "Who cares what he wears under a cap and gown?" Now he is soaked through to the skin. If he were to lie here long enough, would the water penetrate his bones, dilute his blood? He closes his eyes. A lone bird sings, in the deluge.

IV

Susan

1

A few months before Daniel died, a Peace Corps recruiter came to our school. He was ruddy as a ranch hand, and dressed like one—work shirt and blue jeans, hand-tooled leather boots. "I grew up in New York City," he said. "I graduated from Princeton, and I'd probably be a banker by now. But I heard President Kennedy give a speech about the Corps, and it changed my life."

"How?" Daniel said. About thirty of us had gathered in the cafeteria, the recruiter's literature spread out like travel brochures: Africa, South America, Southeast Asia. "How did it change your life?"

I remember how the visitor looked down at his hands,

as if his metamorphosis had been a physical one, as if he were remembering himself before his transformation. "It gave me something to believe in," he said.

"What?" Daniel said. His own hands were folded in his lap, peacefully, I thought then, though now I understand the resignation such a gesture can suggest, and how much anger could have been contained in those clasped palms.

("Bread," Flo had told me, years before. "I believe in bread.")

The recruiter smiled. "America," he said. He flushed like a lover. "I am so damned proud to be an American now."

Each word went up like a flag, red and white and blue, fluttering from porches and poles in a village scene Norman Rockwell might have painted for a cover of *The Saturday Evening Post*. This was 1962. Who knew that a fire ripped through the distant woods, and soon enough the flames would reach the town, and all those billowing flags would burn?

Perhaps Daniel did. He was watching the recruiter wistfully, tenderly, that old man's gaze fixed on the Peace Corps idealist so that it seemed, for a moment, that Daniel was the elder of the two, and too far along in life to summon the hope with which the other shone. If Daniel had lived, I used to think, he would have thrown himself, as I did, into the strife of the sixties—the civil rights struggle and the work against the war in Vietnam galvanizing his energies, focusing his strengths—and I imagined him speaking from podiums all over the country, marching in the front lines, singled out by the swelling crowds who chanted their hero's name: Dan-iel! Dan-iel! Dan-iel!

But now I see how fanciful such speculation was. If he had lived, he might just as well have removed himself from politics entirely, or wound up in Vietnam, enlisting out of his refusal to escape the fate of less fortunate boys

146

for whom student deferments were as remote as space travel, and I might find his name today on the black granite wall—Daniel Rock—one of nearly 50,000 dead in a country the Peace Corps recruiter characterized, that day in the high school cafeteria, as "fluid."

"In this part of the world," he said, turning the globe he had brought with him as a visual aid for his talk, touching his finger to the area around Saigon, "things are very fluid."

"What does that mean?" Daniel had asked, but the Princeton graduate who might have become a banker—may be one today—could not explain.

Susan Perry could not explain Vietnam either, but she had turned the small office we shared in Cleveland's City Hall into a war room: on a huge topographical map that papered the wall beside her drafting table, she tracked with pins the movements of her husband John's platoon. She clipped articles about battles from the *Cleveland Plain Dealer* and posted them every few days on her bulletin board, underlining in red the news she deemed crucial, and photographs of John—on patrol in the Mekong Delta, in a bar in Saigon, peering out of a trench somewhere near the DMZ—framed the window that overlooked frozen Lake Erie, thousands of miles from the steamy Tonkin Gulf.

She sent John samples of the brochures we designed—Susan did the graphics for the copy I wrote. Two young white women working for the first black mayor in America. "What You Need to Know About Rat Control"; "The Facts About Lead Poisoning"; "Are Your Kids on Drugs?" John would answer, "Napalm works real well on rats over here," and, "One nice thing about living in a hooch is that since the walls aren't painted, you don't have to worry about lead. Maybe you could get City Hall to tear down all those slum buildings and put up hooches," and, "I'm sure glad you're getting all those high school kids off drugs, because when we get back to the World, there won't be enough good stuff to go around for everybody."

"He's real funny," Susan would say, reading me John's letters. The pages would tremble in her ink-stained hands. "Isn't he?"

She was nineteen years old. She was five feet tall, but her tininess suggested a kind of strength—the ability to squeeze through narrow passageways and dank underground tunnels, or a talent for scaling walls, her wiry limbs agile as a squirrel's. One might have described her face as angelic—the perfect features, the flawless skin, the white-blond hair like light itself—except for that nervous alertness that gave her always the expression of a chased animal, cunning and corrupted and sad. She dressed like a gypsy—flowing print skirts, gauzy blouses edged with sequins and beads, huge hoop earrings, jangling bracelets—and this added to the impression of tenacious vulnerability, this set her apart, as if, like a true gypsy, she came from a line devoted to dispossession. I sensed she lived already outside the premises that others more cautious (myself among them) were dismantling carefully, one by one, like cars we might someday want to reassemble and drive off in again.

I had a master's in English now. My husband had just graduated from law school and was working for "a liberal firm." Our apartment was furnished in teakwood and rya rugs and prints from retrospectives we had not seen. I could spend a Saturday morning in Hough, one of a squad of volunteers registering black voters in "the Projects," wending my way through those towering new tenements already deteriorating—buckling wallboard, backed-up plumbing, incinerators spewing smoke into the hallways—as if the construction carried within it the confusion and anger of the people who lived there, pain built into the architectural renderings, stirred into the concrete, carried through the pipes and the wiring. At noon, I would drive my Volvo out of Hough, through University Circle, up Cedar Hill into the suburbs, where soon we would move from our modest apartment into a brick Colonial on a parklike lot, and I would stop at the McCarthy-for-President Headquarters in Cleveland Heights, a small storefront sandwiched between a dry cleaner's and a bakery. I had a desk there, and an unsalaried title—Ohio Press Secretary—and later that month I would squire the Minnesota senator through the wards of Cleveland and the suburban shopping malls, and I would fend off reporters crowded around the door to his downtown hotel suite.

"I don't believe in politics," Susan said, when I asked her to join the Voter Registration drive, or McCarthy's campaign.

"You work for Carl Stokes," I said. "Your husband's in Vietnam."

She shrugged. "Well, that's just my little life," she said. "My job and my old man."

"I'm talking about history," I said.

Susan Perry grinned. "I don't believe in that either." She slid off her drafting stool and I thought she might dance, she was so animated now. "I dropped acid the other night and do you know what I saw? Spacemen! Really! I mean, like this is just one silly little planet and if we don't like the way things are turning out, we can just go somewhere else! Right? We can start all over again, right?"

Well, what was that, a childish utterance or a radical manifesto, a drug-induced hallucination or a cosmic insight?

"Maybe so," I said, not meaning it, yet aware of a certain relief as I spoke the words, strange images stirring in that calm pocket, as if I were the one who had swallowed a mind-altering pill.

No one starts over again: I should have told her that. Memory is the soul's metabolism, time the food we eat to live, our daily bread gulped whole, broken down, stored and spent, stored and spent.

"We can start all over again, right?" Susan Perry said.

I did not know then how desperate she was to prove true that wrong-headed giddy hope.

2

"We can start all over again, right?" Joe Perry said to his wife.

She was in Susan's room, packing the girl's belongings. She had emptied the dresser and the closet and the French provincial desk she'd bought Susan five years ago for her tenth birthday—the desk drawers were full of crayon drawings, pencil sketches, watercolors Susan used to paint on the pieces of cardboard that the Chinese laundry put in her father's shirts. Now she used good paper from an art supplies store. Now she used India ink, pastels, tubes of acrylics, and good sable brushes. Joe Perry threw his cardboard inserts away. "One thing you can say about these gooks," he liked to muse, "they do a good shirt."

He was a builder, his father's one-man remodeling business parlayed by the son into construction, Perry Homes all over northern Ohio now. Joe built his wife and daughter a lakefront house in Bratenahl, a thin finger of Cleveland wealth resting on Erie's shore, Russian freighters and cargo barges and fishing trawlers dotting the water beyond the Perrys' yard. Joe Perry liked to sit in a lawn chair and fix his binoculars on the boats. It was almost as if he owned them, the way he could pull them into his line of vision, as if the routes they took were determined now by Joe

150

Perry's will, the captains consulting him instead of their navigational maps.

"No," Sylvia Perry said. She was packing the trunk with one hand and wiping her eyes with a tissue she held in the other. "We're not starting over again anymore."

Although he stood a few feet from her, although he did not need binoculars to see the tears, the puffy cheeks, the nose red from hours of crying, he heard in her voice the quality of distance, as if she were already gone, as if the packing were completed and she had already called the taxi, taken Susan out of school in the middle of the morning, and traveled with her from the terraced lawns of Bratenahl to Norwood's front stoops and tiny row-house yards, all the storefront signs in Hungarian and English, the neighborhood streets fragrant with sauer-kraut and strudel. Joe Perry knew his wife would go to her mother's—the women talked every day, sometimes twice, and whenever Joe brought up the possibility of moving to Texas, where he sensed the next construction boom would be, where he loved the weather, where the women walked around in shorts all year long, Sylvia said flatly she could never leave her mother, never—and he saw Sylvia changing now into the girl he had wooed, sixteen years of marriage shed like a dress she had never liked, the woman's makeup scrubbed from the face still a child's after all, still "a little girl with great big tits;" that was how he'd described her to his bowling team, the night he'd had that run of strikes.

"Well, I guess I won't fight you, then," he said, pushing his bulk off the doorframe of his daughter's room with the ease of a diver releasing himself happily into the water.

Had she actually lived with the man for sixteen years? When he closed the door, he seemed to take time with him, and she wandered the rooms of their luxurious house

151

with a stranger's bewilderment: Where am I? Whose things are these? She did not recognize the Oriental rugs, the Stiffel lamps, the Chippendale tables, or the sofas covered in imported Italian brocade as her own. In the kitchen, she fingered the blender, the built-in dishwasher, the oven built into the wall: what kind of woman cooked in such an elegant workshop? Above the stainless-steel sink, a shelf of cookbooks: *The Perfect Party Planner, Recipes from Cordon Bleu, Gourmet Cuisine.* Some fancy lady had dog-eared the pages of favorite dishes, and none of them sounded like anything Sylvia had ever tasted.

Upstairs, she finished packing Susan's belongings, and then she filled a suitcase with some of her own clothes. She could have a been a thief stealing a wardrobe, for all the familiarity her own garments held for her. In the mirror over her dresser, she stared at herself—a pretty woman with a blond bouffant, even features, nice straight teeth, blue eyes swollen from crying—and Sylvia Perry reached toward the image with her hand, as if to comfort the woman whose drawers she had just rifled.

A taxi took her to Susan's school, a private academy for girls whose grounds were called a "campus" and whose cathedral-like buildings Joe Perry named "the nunnery," though he liked people to know he could afford to send his daughter to such an expensive and prestigious place. It was nearly noon. Sylvia had the driver drop her at the gate. "Wait here," she said. "I have to get my daughter." Snow glazed the lawn and concrete walks and the brooding faces of stone-carved gargoyles whose bodies seemed to be the buildings to which they were affixed. She trembled. Elms and maples rose around her like white ghost trees, and when she looked through the snow-shielded branches to the gray winter sky, she could not imagine sunlight breaking through such bleakness ever again.

"We've had a tragedy in the family," Sylvia said. She

152

was in the office now, speaking to the headmistress's secretary, a thin, formal woman who grasped her desk as Sylvia spoke, as if to brace herself for the terrible news Sylvia would surely describe to her in detail.

"My husband is . . . gone," was all Sylvia said.

The secretary paled. "Mrs. Perry," she said. "Mrs. Perry. Oh, I am—"

"So if you would get Susan out of her class," Sylvia said, "I would be grateful." Her voice lost more volume with each word, no sound accompanying "grateful" at all.

Waiting, Sylvia paced the office. She had been in this room a year ago, when she had brought Susan for an admissions interview with the headmistress. Had these antiques been here then? This velvet settee with the elaborate scrollwork on its mahogany legs, the butler's table on which pieces of Chinese porcelain were displayed, the parchment screen and the hammered brass lamps? She placed her hands on each piece, as if the objects themselves contained her memory of them, and by touching them she could restore to herself their place in her imagination. But she felt nothing, remembered nothing; she was not sure how she had even known the name of the school, which she'd had to tell to the taxi driver when he'd asked her, "Where to, lady?"

"Where to, lady?" He said it again, when she got back in the cab with Susan.

"Will you tell me what's going on?" Susan said.

Sylvia spoke her mother's address, the address of her own childhood. She recognized Susan as her daughter, but otherwise the woman could not recall anything that had happened to her beyond her life in that narrow rowhouse, the bushels of ironing that her mother took in lined up like strange-colored shrubs along the living room wall.

"What's going on?" Susan said. "Is it Dad or Grandma? Is somebody hurt or what?"

"Just give me a minute, dear," Sylvia Perry said, pretending she needed time to compose herself, taking her daughter's hand for comfort but thinking, How could I be old enough to have a child her age?

Behind them, the school receded. They passed their street, but it was barely visible to them, the taxi's windows sleet-blurred now, a stranger driving them through a featureless landscape, landmarks lost, the map of the world as they knew it gone, as if it had never existed.

"Mom, please, I said is somebody—"

And that was the moment, Susan would tell me years later, that was the exact instant in which the bulletin broke into the jazz music to which the driver had been listening, the announcer's voice all but screaming, "The President's been shot, ladies and gentlemen—oh, my God—President John Kennedy's just been shot!"

In her grandmother's tiny living room, the television glowed like a funeral pyre around which the tribal members gathered. For four days they huddled there. They ladled cabbage soup from the kettle Eva Nagy kept warm on the stove and set the bowls they hardly touched on the metal TV tables opened before them. They nursed ginger ale and tea. The hospital vigil, the announcement of the death, the lying-in-state, Oswald's murder, the President's funeral cortege, the burial at Arlington—Susan entered the screen's terrible imagery with the surrender a dreamer offers to her own dreams, however horrific, the mind willingly mired in the archetypal swamp, the waking self submerged in the teeming primal mud. Once, emerging from the trance in which her grandmother and mother remained, Susan called the Bratenahl house: the phone number seemed to her a hieroglyph from an ancient world, and in knowing it, she amazed herself. Her father was not there; that did not amaze, and the pain she'd suffered in the past—"He's gone off with one of his girlfriends," her mother would tell her bluntly, or "He's on a binge," or "He's probably flown down to Houston again" — opened like a chronic sore, and the petite blond teenager with the talent for art placed the receiver down quietly, as if the slightest noise might disturb the wounded in her midst.

"We live here now," Sylvia said, in somnambulistic hush. Moments before, Jackie Kennedy had lit the Eternal Flame on her husband's grave.

"I know that," Susan said. If a single shot had shattered that perfect family, if History itself had fallen into pieces on Friday, how could she presume that her own small life might remain intact? "I know that."

"Who would think this could happen in America?" Eva said. Her accent seemed thicker than it had been, as if she, like Sylvia, had been pitched back in time and she, like Sylvia, was a young girl again herself, the long journey just finished from the Budapest countryside, from her father's blighted orchard, her mother's failing health. Her fingers moved like a blind woman's over the rosary beads entwined in her hands for four days now. "Who would think I would see such a thing in this country?"

Susan finished high school at Our Lady of Lourdes, three blocks from her grandmother's, where she slept in the attic, the sloped walls on either side of her single bed covered with her paintings, sketches, pastel drawings, pen-and-ink designs. She made a few new friends, but mostly she kept to herself. She did not date; she said she had a boyfriend from Bratenahl, in college now in California, and she carried a picture of a cousin in her wallet and said he was "my steady." She believed the lie a little herself, and the fantasy protected her from the knowledge of her loneliness. She was absent from her own life. Sometimes she wondered where Susan Perry was, as if she were thinking about another girl entirely, someone she had known in her old life, someone who had moved, suddenly, without leaving a phone number or a forwarding address. She never set foot in the Bratenahl house again. Joe Perry put it up for sale, and one of his construction workers brought the rest of her belongings, and her mother's, to Eva's one day in a Perry Homes pickup truck. Joe moved into the penthouse at Lakeside Towers downtown, and occasionally Susan had dinner there, Chinese food they ate from the cartons at Joe's glass-topped table, the thronelike chairs covered in textured red velvet.

Once she asked him, "What do you think of Martin Luther King?" and he said, "I think a pretty little white girl shouldn't have the colored on her mind, is what I think."

She stood in the doorway to her mother's room. A fan on the floor billowed the sheet up over her legs, so that Sylvia seemed to be in some sort of oxygen tent, although her face was visible and she appeared to be breathing on her own.

"You asleep?"

Sylvia shook her head from side to side, but kept her eyes shut. Susan sat gingerly on the bed's edge.

"I got accepted," she said. "To the Cleveland Art Institute."

Sylvia smiled, raised her lids with effort. "Oh, that's nice." Her voice was tired and small.

"I start right after Labor Day, and I want—"

"Please don't bounce like that, honey. My stomach is so upset today."

How many days a week did she spend in bed now, with stomachaches and headaches and fevers no doctor could explain?

"I'll get you an Alka-Seltzer," Susan said.

"They don't help me."

Susan looked at her mother's face and saw her own there: the deep-set blue eyes, the straight nose, the pretty mouth, the clear white skin almost transparent across the brow, as if the faintest touch there might leave a bruise.

"Well, Mom, what I want to ask you is—"

Sylvia Perry shut her eyes again. "Not now, dear. I don't like to make decisions when I'm not feeling well."

"What I fail to understand," Joe Perry said, "is why she doesn't get herself a job." He laced his shrimp chop suey with soy sauce. "Get herself out of that damn house. Your grandmother has her going to mass twice a day now, did you know that?"

"She turned into a little girl again," Susan said. "She regressed."

"Where you learning shrink talk? In my book, that's as bad as the old lady's Hail Marys."

"I read about it in a magazine," Susan said. She split open her egg roll with her fork. "Anyhow, I don't want to talk about them. I just want to know if you'll give me rent money for an apartment."

"Your mother will have my ass."

She put her palms on the table. "I need to get out of there."

"I can understand that," Joe Perry said. He swigged down his tea. "I sure can understand that." He shoveled the last of his fried rice into his mouth. "You got to hand it to these gooks, they can cook."

That summer Hough burned. For five days, the ghetto glowed like a cinder consuming itself with its own heat. Although they lived miles from the conflagration, Eva bought more locks for the doors and slept with a hammer underneath her bed. Sylvia wanted the three of them to drive downstate to Yellow Springs, where they had cousins, but Eva refused to leave the house to the looters she knew would spill into the white neighborhoods once they had ravaged their own.

157

"Nobody's going to bother us here," Susan said.

"This is a child speaking," her grandmother said, as if to God. "In Europe we had riots, and I am telling you a man doesn't carry a torch in one hand and a map in another. They burn wherever. Wherever."

But Susan stared at the faces on the nightly news footage and saw in the eyes of the cursing men something resigned, still, sadder than revenge required. They were like the monks who were setting themselves afire in Vietnam. Maybe after Hough's buildings burned, these men, too, would pour gasoline on themselves and join the immolated Buddhists in another world.

"Well, I think you're wrong," Susan said. "I don't think they'll come here at all."

On Monday of Labor Day Weekend, 1966, Eva Nagy fit four heavyweight paper plates into rattan holders, counted out plastic forks and spoons, and took jelly glasses down from the cupboard. She held them up to the sunlight, checking for streaks.

"Ach," she said. "This hard water here. Rinse these out again."

Sylvia looked up from the cucumber she was slicing into translucent wafers. She held the knife in midair for a moment, then set it down and turned on the faucet. The water belched out brown, rattling the pipes. She turned off the tap. "It's rusty," she said. "I can't."

Eva Nagy sighed again. "I'll pour in the lemonade before he comes. So he won't notice the streaks."

Sylvia picked up her knife again. "He wouldn't notice."

"Oh, sure," the old woman said. "That's how you think." She loaded a tray with the paper plates and plastic utensils and the glasses. "Listen to me: a man likes things nice even if he can't make nice by himself. Maybe you'd still have a husband if—"

158

"Stop it! Stop it right now! Why do you take his side? I'm your own daughter. Why—"

"Who cares for sides? I'm not talking sides. You got married in the church. It's a sacrament."

"You'll make me sick again."

Eva went out the back door. Sylvia stood at the window, chewing her lip, watching her mother spread a cloth on the weathered picnic table that filled up most of the stamp-size yard. Then she yanked down the shade, blocking the strong noon rays. In the dimness, she turned back to the salad she was making.

"It's dark in here," Susan said. She had come down from her bedroom, where she'd packed the last of her things. "How come you're working in the dark?"

Sylvia ripped up more lettuce. "My head hurts."

"I don't doubt it." She picked out a piece of tomato with her fingers. "This picnic is the dumbest—"

Sylvia Perry wheeled around. "He didn't have to accept. He could have said no when she called him. He could have—"

"My father is not the kind of man who turns down a free meal from anyone. Is he?"

Sylvia massaged her temples with her fingers. "You know what he's like. You know exactly what he's like, and you still let him talk you into—"

"He didn't talk me into anything. Moving is my own idea. He didn't even want—"

"He didn't even want to be your father!" Sylvia screamed. "He never wanted you and now he's taking you away from me!"

Eva Nagy rushed in from outside. "Stop it! Shame on the both of you! No fighting today, do you hear me? Do you hear?"

Susan Perry stuck her fingers in her ears. "No," she said. "I don't hear a thing." She drifted out the door into the shimmering yard.

Eva snapped up the shade. "A beautiful day. Look. Can't you see what a beautiful day is there?"

At four o'clock, Joe Perry drove his daughter from her grandmother's house to her new apartment, a furnished flat on the edge of University Circle, a twenty-minute walk to the Art Institute.

"Two crazy dames," he said. He took a last deep drag of his cigarette and pitched the butt out the car window. "Crazier than bedbugs, those two."

Susan said nothing. She pushed in the lighter on the dashboard and lit her own Salem with the red-hot coil.

Joe eyed her. "Since when you smoke."

Susan exhaled. "Since I moved."

He set his hand on his daughter's thigh. "You're a real little terror, aren't you?" he said. His hand drifted to the radio and turned up the volume.

"Not really," Susan said, but her words were lost in the music's din.

"Home sweet home," Joe Perry said finally, pulling up in front of a brown brick building on a street of identical structures. "One thing you don't get in apartment living is flags on holidays. Ever notice that? People who live in apartments don't fly flags."

Susan opened the car door. "I think I can stand it," she said.

"I guess you'll have to," Joe Perry said and got out his side.

It took them each several trips up and down to move her into the three furnished rooms. Three suitcases, seven cardboard cartons, a Styrofoam cooler filled with perishables her mother gathered together at the last minute, a portable record player, and a large portfolio containing her work. When they finished, Joe sprawled on the frayed Colonial print couch. Susan stretched out on the braided rug; her sweat sank into the loops.

160

"Don't suppose your mother stuck a few beers in that cooler," Joe said to the ceiling.

"Orange juice and buttermilk."

"You ever had beer?"

"Twice."

"You like it?"

"Not much."

"You'll learn to." He rose up on an elbow, lit a cigarette, offered her one from his pack.

"No, thanks," Susan said. "I better put that food away."

In the kitchen, she poured the buttermilk into the sink and drank some orange juice out of the jar.

"Gimme some juice then," Joe Perry hollered from the other room.

She brought him what was left and he gulped it down. He handed her the empty bottle. "I guess I'll push off. Anything else you need?"

She put the cold glass up against her cheek. "No," she said. "I don't need anything at all."

When she felt cooler and less nervous, she ate a ham sandwich and a half of a cantaloupe. Then she unpacked her things. Once her clothes were hanging in the closet and stacked in neat piles in the dresser drawers, the place seemed less strange. Still, she could not believe she lived here now. Three years ago, when they had left the house in Bratenahl and moved in with her grandmother, Susan had wandered the rooms for weeks. She had memorized furniture—the slipcover patterns, the grain of the wood, the scratches and burns her grandmother tried to conceal with shoe polish and doilies she crocheted herself. From every window, Susan had sketched the terrain—the small yard shaded by an elm taller than the rowhouse itself, her grandmother's garden plot, wisteria fanned out along the metal fence, narrow bricked street out front, the buckling sidewalk scrubbed clean each day by Eva and her neighbors, old women in babushkas and cotton housedresses conversing in Hungarian. At night in her bed, she would study the drawings she'd made as if they were x-rays and she a doctor stymied by a difficult case. Often she'd stayed awake until morning, listening, as if to an irregular pulse, to the unfamiliar noises in the walls and the pipes.

Now, in this apartment, she shoved the empty suitcases under the bed. In the living room, she found the box that contained sheets, blankets, and a foam rubber pillow (she was allergic to feathers). When the bed was made, she flattened all the empty boxes and carried them down the hallway to the incinerator room. Behind other doors, she heard rock music, and Dylan, and Lyndon Johnson's press conference. "General Westmoreland assures me that another five thousand will turn the tide," the President drawled, "and I trust his assessment entirely." How could Lyndon Johnson trust anyone, after November 22, 1963? She remembered how he had looked on Air Force One, his hand on the Bible, his face a crushed mask. Didn't he spend every moment waiting for a shot aimed at him? Didn't everyone? Who could ever be at home again anywhere? Wasn't everyone ready all the time to duck, to flee, to disappear?

She shut the iron door on the last carton. She lived here now; those burning boxes attested to that. She felt as if she had completed some ritual in a ceremony she could not name. She was halfway down the hall when black smoke poured from the incinerator room and she joined the strangers fleeing the sudden storm of ashes and fumes, as if they'd been driven outside by a fire. ("It happens all the time," another tenant told her. "The chute's too narrow, things get stuck, and before you know it we're all out here on the sidewalk.") In the humid dusk, she waited with the others for the super to call them back inside. They offered their names to her. She gave them her own. Her

mother might be lying down with a washcloth over her
eyes; her father might be fixing himself another martini
while one of his girlfriends sat naked on his bed and polished her toenails frosted magenta; her grandmother might
be lighting candles in church for all their threatened souls.
Well, what they did meant nothing to Susan Perry anymore. No. She had left one world and entered another.
Those were not cartons she had burned, that was her past,
eighteen years of memories blazing and smoking like a
bomb's aftermath.

"We can start all over again, right?" she had asked me.
I should have told her what a lie that was, but I was
not sure enough myself, and her incandescence dazzled
me: how could I have known she was burning herself
alive?

3

They liked to turn out all the lights, she
told me, and watch the reefer glow.
They liked to listen to Ravi Shankar while they
screwed.
They liked to drink beer in a bar in "the Flats," that
neighborhood of stevedores and steelworkers and some
students like Susan and John, who came there for "the
color," they said, and because it was cheap.
They liked to take their sketch pads to Rockefeller
Park, and sometimes they liked to go downtown and draw
"all those weirdos"—the bag ladies and the self-styled

preachers and the man who thought he was one of the pigeons that gathered to feed in Public Square.

They planned to be famous artists, she told me, move to California and live in a cliffside house overlooking the Pacific. But first he had to come home from "the war," she said, as if there were a place with precisely that name, as if all the battles ever fought and all the bombs dropped and all the civilians buried in the huge pits that pocked the earth were located in one tiny spot on the planet.

When she told me her husband had enlisted—they'd married a week after they'd met in a watercolor class, run off together to a justice of the peace in Wheeling, West Virginia, and John had moved out of the apartment he shared with three other students and into Susan's place— I said, "Did you know I'm working for Senator McCarthy? I'm really against this war, Susan."

"Oh, so is John!" she said, as if happily discovering another compatriot.

"But he enlisted," I said. "He wasn't even drafted. He gave up his defer—"

"Well, see, like his brother was drafted—he was a plumber, like their dad—and, well, he was killed there. So I mean, what else could John do? I mean, he didn't think it was fair for Billy to go over there and get himself blown away and John gets to—like, it doesn't have any-thing to do with the war, really. It's a family thing."

She wanted my assent, she wanted my verification of her logic. She reminded me of my mother holding up an afghan she was working on: "See, I made up my own pattern. It's not bad, is it? I had so many little pieces of yarn in the house, I just. . . . Do you think the colors go? It's not too busy, is it? I think it's nice, you get tired of squares and stripes anyhow."

What could I say? The colors clashed, which my mother knew. Being in Vietnam had everything to do with the war, which Susan knew.

"It's interesting," I had said to my mother.

To Susan, I said, "Life can get very confusing," and I saw the tears flood her eyes, and we both went back to our work.

Beside the map of Vietnam, she pinned a gallery of photographs to the bulletin board. John in their apartment, John on the ferryboat the time they took a trip to Kelley's Island, John in basic training, John in Hawaii before he was shipped overseas and she'd begged her father for money to visit him there. "This is Kilauea," she told me, pointing to the picture of Hawaii's live volcano, fountains of fire rising into the air, John leaning over the roped-off sightseeing ledge as if preparing for a plunge into the lava burning below. "Don't you love it?" I said I found his pose a little frightening, but she laughed at me. "You don't understand what a cutup he is."

From Vietnam, he sent her pictures of his platoon and a few of himself: putting on his flak jacket, cleaning his gun, posing like a conqueror on top of an armored tank. I saw how old he had become in the few short months he had been there, his boyish features toughened, his open grin turned into a smile tight and covert, his soft eyes glassy-hard. Did Susan see the change in him? If he was aging in a way that frightened her, she herself seemed to be getting younger and younger each day of his absence. She would come in late to work and claim she had forgotten to set her alarm, or had missed the bus, or slept past her stop. The sleepiness was true: she developed dark circles under her eyes, alarming against her alabaster skin, and finally she started mentioning parties on week nights and barhopping into the morning and someone named Amos ("Amos says I look like Sandra Dee. Who's Sandra Dee?" or "Amos knows the coolest card tricks. I swear, he's supernatural!"). She failed to make deadlines on projects—the layout for a brochure, the lettering on a poster mock-up set to go that day to the printer, the drawing of children's faces for the Report of the Mayor's Commission on Elementary Education in the City of Cleveland. "It's this allergy," she'd say, her eyes red, her nose always running, her voice hoarse or squeaky but rarely her own anymore, as if another person were inhabiting her body.

"What do you hear from John?" I would ask her, because she had stopped reading me his letters.

"Oh, you know," she would say, not meeting my eyes. "Stuff."

This is what I did not know:

That John was missing in action.

That Eddie Jackson, the chief housing inspector whose office was downstairs from us, who wandered in to visit Susan three and four and five times a week, telling jokes, flirting, passed her small white envelopes I pretended not to see, or saw without realizing what they contained: heroin.

That Amos was a pimp for whom she worked in order to support her addiction; her pallor and her weight loss and her constantly runny nose—obvious symptoms I failed to recognize. Did I blind myself, too, to the needle marks on her fragile arms? Oh, I had such a feel in those days for global disasters, social ills. I had the statistics and the pending legislation and the moral arguments down pat, I understood the history of my time in the way I might have studied solid geometry: a series of proofs to be mastered, complicated diagrams I could learn to draw myself. But in the presence of a single self-destructive girl whose pain must have filled our office like the smell of rotting fruit, I missed the simplest clues.

That Charles Whitney, Susan's boss and mine, a former disk jockey on one of the city's black radio stations ("an ineffectual administrator," some management consultant would later conclude, "a patronage appointment of the worst sort"), knew for months what I, who sat three feet from her, ignored; that he kept her on the payroll; that he went to her apartment many times and threw out the "tricks" and threw out her needles and told Amos that he, Charles Whitney, "don't give a shit how many cops you're paying off, I'll get you busted yet, you goddam son of a bitch," and took her to the hospital, from which she always checked out as soon as he left her there alone.

That Joe Perry had moved to Houston.

That Sylvia Perry never got out of bed anymore.

That Eva Nagy wrote her granddaughter a letter that said, in crippled scrawl, *You will burn in Hell for what you done. Not to be married in the Church. Little Susie, why why why?*

Once I invited her to dinner, after work.

"To your house?" she said. "With your husband?"

She looked as if I had offered her a gift she had neither expected nor coveted, and did not exactly know how to use, but which touched her nonetheless.

"I don't know," she said. "I've been tired—"

"You're really run-down," I said. I was proofing the copy on a flyer for which she'd just finished the layout. The office smelled of rubber cement and marking-pen ink. "You probably don't eat right, living by yourself, do you?"

I was newly pregnant, and all my impulses were maternal now.

"Well, I'm not hungry much," she said, forcing herself to smile. "Have to keep my girlish figure, right?"

"Oh, don't worry," I said, the banter stretched like gauze over some nameless wound. "One plate of spaghetti won't kill you."

When she was gone, Aaron said, "Christ, she's flaky." He was packing a suitcase for a business trip the next morning to Washington, D.C. "How do you take all those hours with her?"

"I don't mind her," I said. We were in our new house now, in the master bedroom with its own bath and the two walk-in closets. "I like her. She's a talented girl."

He shrugged. "Whatever you say, sweetheart." He got under the covers and put his hand on my belly. "How's Junior?" he said into my ear, and turned out the light.

Afterward, Aaron slipped easily into sleep; he was an untroubled man for whom my bouts of sadness and anxiety were inexplicable and threatening. Aaron claimed not to dream—"You mean you don't remember your dreams," I would say, and he would tell me, "No, I mean I don't have any dreams. When I sleep, I sleep"—and when I told him this was scientifically impossible, he said, "I know what goes on in my own head better than some grad student in Clinical Voodoo who counts the number of times somebody's eyelids twitch and calls that science." For a long time, I would take refuge in his skepticism. I wanted to live on the smooth surface he claimed to inhabit even at night, his world windless and flat and free of the fault-line I sensed beneath my own studied poise.

Now I listened to his even breathing, and I heard again his indictment of Susan—"Christ, she's flaky. How do you take all those hours with her?"—and I realized the censure had been directed as much at me as at her, the scorn a man might have for two sisters who, however different they might appear from each other, share the bonds of memory and blood, recognize themselves in the other, and discover in that mirroring an intimacy the man cannot enter or understand. Until I had invited Susan home, she seemed utterly unlike me, but in Aaron's presence, in the glare of his lawyerly scrutiny, in his defensive dismissal of her and of me, I sensed for the first time how much we resembled each other, Susan and I, two injured children pretending to be grown, siblings of a sort, grief-fed American girls lying awake in the same ghostly dark.

I eased myself from the bed. I walked down the plushly carpeted stairs to the kitchen. I heated some milk and sipped it, hoping to settle the waves of distress that rose from belly to throat. It was the baby, I told myself, though I had not had any discomforts before, not even the morning sickness for which I had prepared myself with boxes of soda crackers I could eat before rising, until the nausea subsided. Well, this was nausea, but not from the baby I carried. My own roiling history loosened in me, another kind of labor just beginning, to last for a decade, until finally—my marriage over, my daughter turned ten, my memory reclaimed, my stories arriving like once-censored dreams—I would give birth to my own life.

I sat in the kitchen for hours that night. I studied it the way I have pictured Susan's mother studying her own on the day her husband left her: Who lives here? Whose palace is this? That had been my mother's word for this house when Aaron and I had moved in and my parents had come to Cleveland from Pittsburgh to visit for a week. "My daughter lives in a palace," she had said, and I could see she was both pleased and incredulous that I should have moved out of my reclusive, melancholy girlhood into a marriage so worldly and striving and geared toward display. "And working in politics yet," my father had said, as if that were further evidence that I had been transformed, a shy, bookish girl turned feisty and social and shrewd. Why shouldn't they believe I had truly changed? I nearly believed it myself.

Once Susan and I drove together in a city car to Hough. We were going to meet with Jessie Mae Houston, a ward leader close to the Mayor, about materials we were preparing for a meeting between the Model Cities Neighborhood Board and "the Feds" who were flying in later that week from Washington.

"I'd come down to City Hall," Jessie Mae had told me

on the phone, "except I don't got no one to leave in the shop here."

We rode past riot-wrecked buildings still boarded up, the singed bricks and the scorched roofs and the window glass heaped into mounds so that they looked like naturally occurring crystal formations. On the corners, knots of men called to us or followed our progress silently through wine-dazed eyes.

"I could live here," Susan said.

"I don't think that would be a great idea," I said.

"I just meant I could do it," she said.

Jessie Mae had turned the living room of her dilapidated frame house into a beauty parlor: chair-mounted dryers and a sink and a table laden with straightening irons and bobby pins, brushes and combs, jars of pomade and a pan of lye simmering on a hot plate. Even in the kitchen, to which she led us for our "conference," the odor of burning hair—"processed," Blacks called the lye-straightened hair for which they were willing to risk their scalp, their skin, their eyes, their hands—followed us.

"What do I smell?" Susan said.

Jessie Mae had just spread her folders on the table and gotten out her yellow legal pad.

"Oh, that's from treatments," she said, as if naming a medicinal procedure.

"What kind of treatments?" Susan said. Did she think the pot of lye was another drug she might try? Did she hope it might be some potion she could drink and John would be back and Amos would die and she would never need another shot of heroin again? Or was she, in spite of her ruin, still a spirit engaged in life, able to reach out with true interest to a woman who happened to be black, while I, in my well-tended health, held back, hedged, kept the distance my politics disavowed?

"Oh, baby," Jessie Mae said. "You are so-o-o-o white, ain't you?"

They roared together, they hugged, they danced together in that kitchen, this hefty black woman with skin the color of coffee and an auburn wig she wore over the Afro she only showed to "brothers and sisters" but not to "downtown white ladies" who "weren't altogether ready for the real Jessie Mae, you know what I mean?" and this tiny blue-eyed blonde whose hair reached her waist when she untwisted it and whose mother used to call her "Rapunzel," that imprisoned beauty whose only escape lay in her own body given painfully to a man.

"Jessie Mae," Susan said, once she had recovered from laughter, "when we finish with our work, could I have an appointment in your shop?"

"In my—?"

"I want you to do my hair in corn rows." She squealed in delight at her own idea. She turned to me. I had smiled through their peals, moved by the ease with which they had summoned each other forth, out of the absurdities of race and time, into easy—enviable—soulful embrace. "You don't mind waiting, do you?"

I shook my head. What I minded was being outside their rapport, but I was not "flaky" enough, or streetwise, or willing yet in my life to step off the earth, in one way or another, risking rebuff or scorn or the hatred History sends through the blood of its children.

"You can watch, missy," Jessie Mae said to me, as if she recognized my loneliness, which I would not have called by that name then, not aware that my girlhood's anguish still lived inside me, as if it were another baby I carried next to the one whose first kicks I felt that afternoon, while Jessie Mae did Susan's hair in corn rows and told her, "You call me Mama from now on, hear?"

In my sixth month, I quit my job at City Hall. Susan gave me a blanket she said had been hers when she was a baby, and when I said, "That is so sweet of you, but wouldn't

171

you want to save it for your own?", she patted my stomach and said, "Well, I just wanted to keep it in the family, big sister," and we both cried a little and said good-bye and of course we'd stay in touch and would she let me know when John got home and I better call her "when the kid comes," and that was the last conversation we ever had.

"Didn't anybody tell you?" our old boss Charles Whitney said. This was a year later, at a cocktail party, a fundraiser for Mayor Stokes, and I had asked Charles how Susan was. "She OD'd, honey. She just couldn't kick it."

Oh, little sister, it is decades later, and I am still trying to dream you alive.

V

Lila

1

Lila Frank lay beside me in the labor room, a curtain drawn between our beds. I did not know her name yet; I did not know we looked enough alike to be taken for sisters. I knew her by her breathing: we had both studied Lamaze, our husbands stood ready with wash-cloths and lollipops and cups of crushed ice. I knew her by the cry that broke a few times through the trained exhalations, the cry of a woman whose bones are moving, a small world shifting from its axis, birth a cosmic exertion after all.

On the maternity ward, we shared a room, our daughters born within minutes of each other, and quickly we recognized one another as the curtained partner with whom we'd shared those hours of struggle and sweat and—how to describe that joyous moment when those tiny heads pushed through?—ecstasy neither of us had ever felt before. The babies came and went, back and forth every four hours from the nursery on dollies that delivered them to us like box lunches, like potted plants—the aides seemed that casual about our infants. We examined them over and over, from head to toe, chanting aloud their markings to them, echoing the sounds they made so that their coos took on a choral stature. We nursed them until they fell asleep, and we taught each other how to wake them up: scratch her heel, tickle her under her chin, switch sides. After they ate, we burped our babies over our shoulders, across our legs, or leaning over, our arms raised like fence rails across their tiny chests. Alone, we tended to our own bodies and suggested remedies to one another—my stitches ached, her breasts became engorged, both of us had hemorrhoids—so that although we were in the hospital, we were practicing also a kind of folk medicine, as if there were a pool of common knowledge on which women draw when they give birth, a legacy we only learn we have at that time. If we had been given straw, Lila and I, we would have built huts side by side and washed our clothes in the river and hauled water in jugs we balanced on our heads. Every day our husbands visited, and family and friends, and Lila and I would realize that we were strangers to each other, each of us embedded in a complicated life of which the other had no knowledge. And yet we would cry on the day we each went home, as if we were leaving a household we loved—fifth floor, A wing, room 725—as if we were truly sisters with a common past, dense and memorable and worthy of grief.

"Hormones," we laughed to each other as we wept, our husbands waiting for us, the nurses dressing each baby in the kimonos and booties their fathers had brought from

176

the nurseries readied weeks ago. Hormones, yes. And history, too: that week together decades long, in a country we had entered together, no map adequate, each of us immigrants, as it were, without possessions, new arrivals like the infants we took to our transformed, milk-throbbing breasts—how strange our own bodies had become to us, how beautiful and foreign this territory of the flesh.

We lived an hour's drive from each other—I in my East Side suburb, Lila on the west side of the Cuyahoga in Rocky River in a four-bedroom Tudor (she was married to a doctor then, an orthopedist with a thriving practice). We visited each other in our homes, and talked on the phone a few times, and went together one night to see *Swan Lake* at Severance Hall; then we let the friendship lapse. Geography, we might have insisted—the long trip across the city—thwarted us. Or perhaps we would have cited certain differences in style: Lila's outspokenness, my increasingly measured manner. I think now it was our closeness we fled, that week in the hospital so charged for us, so intimate, we had felt more married to each other than to our husbands. In each other's company, we had felt disloyal to the men whose children we had borne. I am not speaking here of sex, which has its power, but of other connections, equally strong.

During those years we lost track of each other, Lila would become an increasingly active feminist, organizing for NOW, joining a consciousness-raising group, contemplating more radical political action. Her husband would hate this change in her that he said had begun with her pregnancy, though she fixed the date months after her baby's birth. He wanted her to see an endocrinologist, who would surely "cure" Lila with estrogen or some other compound he would prescribe: her growing militancy would abate like a fever, her feminist diction would be silenced once she healed.

Perhaps all women die to their old lives when a new one grows inside them. I began to write after Beth was born, images dividing again and again like the cells that had formed her body inside my own. Now I spent almost all my time at home, caring for her, and when she slept, I crafted stories emptied of politics, emptied of history; the life I created was like the one I was living myself: insular, unengaged, compendiums of the private. Soon the tales I dreamed on the page made a world richer and more immediate to me than the one my husband Aaron still traveled to each morning, his briefcase stuffed with documents in a language I was fast forgetting.

"Most of the time you're just not here," he would tell me.

Most of the time he was right.

"It's not healthy," he would say. "You're turning back to the way you were when I met you. You're going back into your shell. You were a very outgoing person for a while there. You were involved, for Christ's sake. You liked people. I don't understand why being home with a child should change your entire personality. Maybe you need to go back to work. When's the last time you read the newspaper? When's the last time we had anyone over to dinner, for Christ's sake?"

For days I thought about the shell to which he claimed I was returning. My mother kept one from her childhood on top of her dresser. "You can hear the ocean," she liked to say, holding the spiky conch to her ear. Inside, the shell was skin-smooth, alabaster deepening to pink, and then that darkness the eye could not enter. What would it be like in that roaring sea-filled cave? Like being in a womb again. Like a second birth.

"I need to talk to you," I said to Lila finally, years later, when my marriage was ending, when my loneliness peaked. She was already divorced, living with her daughter in a ramshackle house in the city with several other women "in transition," though I was not sure from what to what.

"Well, I need to talk to you too," she said, and the silence between us fell away and the true conversation—which outlasts death—began.

2

When Lila Shepard Frank was a child, her father taught her how to swim in the Scioto River.

"It's the one thing I remember us doing together," she told me." He didn't mean to ignore me. He just never knew what to say to a daughter."

Thirty miles north of Columbus, the Shepards had a bungalow in the village of Delaware, their three acres thick with maples, white ash, sycamores. Through the trees, Lila could see the river from her room—slivers of blue in the leafy summer branches, icy white wedges between the wintered limbs.

"Don't get her chilled," Alice Shepard said to her husband. "And don't take her out by the rocks, it's too dangerous there."

"I think I can take care of my own kid, Alice," Bill Shepard said.

He looked wounded, but in fact he felt relieved to hear Alice speak out loud what he had always surmised: a girl belonged to her mother, first and foremost, and a man wasn't fully a father until he had a son. Greg Morton at the foundry had just had a boy, and Bill envied Greg the fishing trips, the OSU football games, the Cub Scout outings he would have when the baby was older.

Lila was sitting on the kitchen floor, putting on her sneakers. She was five years old, and her parents talked about her all the time in her presence, as if she were too young to understand what they said, as if they were speaking in a tongue of which she had no knowledge. Or perhaps that seeming indifference to a child's awareness is a masquerade adults perform; perhaps, in fact, they wait for the child to enter the room, perhaps they want the child to overhear the ways in which they struggle for her loyalty and the ways in which they are willing to relinquish it. Understand the issues here, they might be announcing: love is political.

They walked to the water. Lila listened to her father's shoes scrunching the maple pods, spread like gravel over the dirt road by rain the night before. He did not talk, but she was used to his silence. It used to frighten her, his wordlessness opening around him like a trench into which she might slip. She had learned to listen for other sounds he made: footsteps, whistling, cracking his knuckles. Even his breathing became a kind of chatter, unguarded and freely given. If there were no exchange between them at all, how could she trust him? Speech would be easiest—how she sometimes craved her father's talk!—but she could learn his other languages, if that was what was required. If she had to, she could listen to his heartbeat and answer with her own.

She followed him along the shore, past the Slaytons' property, beyond the split-rail fence that marked the Purdys' yard. Now they were at the edge of the lot that sat between the river and the park where the boys played ball on summer nights, a few hitters famous for the home runs they sent sailing past the outfield, over the elephant grass, into the Scioto's moon-glazed depths. Come daylight, local children dove for those balls they believed were buried in the riverbed, but no one ever found the treasure they sought. "Think of it," her father like to muse. "A thousand years from now some archaeologist will dig up one of those homers and put it in a museum in Washington, D.C. That's what they did with the Dead Sea Scrolls."

Now he said, "This is a good place, Lila. Take off your shoes and put them by mine."

It was very early in the morning, not even eight, and the grass was still weighted down with dew. Last night, when he had come up with the idea—"All right," he had said, as if resolving some long debate of which she had not been aware, "I guess we better teach you how to swim properly, safety rules and all, now that you're going off on your own with the others to play"—Lila had looked to her mother for some clue about how she, the daughter, should feel.

"That's a wonderful idea," Alice Shepard had said, but fear trembled at the edges of her smile.

("She was afraid of him," Lila would tell me years later, remembering.

"Was he abusive?"

"He didn't have to be," she said. "He was male.")

That night Lila hardly slept. She had swallowed her mother's anxiety like a pill with her peas, and now it roiled inside her, a confusion she could not name. Why was her father going to give her swimming lessons? When had he ever suggested an outing together, just the two of them? What had he ever taught her himself? From her mother, she had learned her letters, printing her name, how to tie her shoes, the way to roll out piecrust dough, good manners. It was Alice who had taken her to the intersection by the elementary school and made her practice crossing the street twenty times: waiting for the green light, looking right and left, walking briskly through the crosswalk from one curb to the other. Who had taught her how to ride a bike? Her mother. Who explained God to her, and Me-

181

morial Day, and the Fourth of July? Her mother, too. Perhaps Lila was betraying Alice by even agreeing to go with Bill, let alone feeling pleased about it, excited, as if it were her birthday. None of these notions had words attached to them; they floated in and out of her mind like the shadows that gathered and broke on the wall facing her bed.

Now she bent over and undid her laces. The lot looked like a huge prism, each shimmering blade a facet in which her face danced. Her father pulled his jersey over his head and the shining grass caught his motion. Changed to light, relieved of their bodies, Lila might have been watching their souls skimming over the earth. She felt a rush of pure love for the man. He was going to teach her how to swim! She was entrusting her life to him, and he wanted the offering; he had asked for it himself. "I think I know how to take care of my own kid," he'd told her mother, and Lila let that protestation encircle her like the tube he was inflating now, puffs of his own breath promising her safety. On the fringes of her awareness—as if in a tree, or downriver where the rocks glinted—her mother's uneasiness flashed.

He pulled the plastic ring over her upraised arms, past her shoulders to her waist. "Okay," he said, "let's go in."

He was running ahead of her into the water. Her mother would have taken her hand. Her mother would have led her slowly, inch by inch, from the shore to the dip several feet out where the river deepened some, but Bill Shepard took that shallow span in three leaps and stood in water up to his waist before Lila had taken a single step off land. Her feet were mired in the marshy earth.

"C'mon," he said. He was facing her. "It's nice and warm."

"I'm scared," she said.

Was that true? Hadn't she loved the sight of her father galloping so easily from one element to another he seemed amphibian? Even as she was wishing for her mother's cautious guidance, wasn't Lila laughing out loud at her father's antic splashes, didn't her own body feel springy as a diver's at the sight of Bill Shepard's bravura? She wanted to find the place in the air through which he had charged, she wanted to follow his movements as if he had made a dance for her, as if he were Miss Bennett in ballet class showing the girls their first arabesques and grands jetés.

But she said, "I'm scared, Daddy," again, the words not so much her own as ones she had learned somewhere, had been taught to honor, like the Pledge of Allegiance she had just mastered in school, or the Lord's Prayer she said with her mother every night before bed. Fear was her duty, the child sensed, and Lila was dutiful.

He waded back.

"I guess I forgot you're a girl," he said, rebuking them both.

"I guess so," Lila said, the gulf between them opening again, wide as the Scioto.

For years she would dream that she had flown after him, her feet finding his path through the water from shore to shoulder-high depth, her female laughter rising to the tops of the sun-crystalled trees, his arms open to catch his spunky daughter, brave as any boy, adventurous and strong.

"Here," he said, "give me your hand," and he led her in by inches.

When he had her in water up to her waist, he stopped abruptly. She looked up at him, and though she had to squint, she could see the puzzle his face had become, as if not even his own features made sense to him now, as if, for a moment, the logic of muscles and nerves had deserted him. Did he recognize her? His eyes registered an amnesiac's bewilderment, or the confusion of a man in strange territory to which he has been consigned without a compass, without a map. How should I proceed? he seemed to be asking her. Tell me what to do next.

"Daddy," Lila said, reminding him of his relation to her.

As if the appellation were a hazy landmark that had risen in the distance, he took a deep breath of the less-alien air.

"Let's go in a little deeper," he said, his voice quavering, and they resumed their tentative and careful pace.

Farther in, he told her, "This is good," and though he did not sound as certain as the words implied, he seemed to gain courage once they were said.

He held his arms like a raft extending from his body. "Lie across here," he said, and when he saw Lila hesitate, he told her, "When I was a high school boy, I used to give lessons for pay. I taught a lot of kids your age to swim, right in this river."

She stretched out across her father's rigid arms. Water lapped at her chin, her toes. He instructed her well, as a teacher might, because it was his job. By week's end, she could do the backstroke and the crawl, and before summer was over she would be diving with the others, looking for homers that the boys hit out of the ball field, over the vacant lot, into the river where—local legend notwith-standing—the current would have carried them far away from Delaware, Ohio, into the teeming world.

Alice Shepard was seventeen when she met Bill, nineteen when they married. Her maiden name was Kreuger, her parents German immigrants who lived with their five children in a two-bedroom apartment in Columbus, directly above their dry-goods store. Every day after school, Alice, the eldest, took her mother's place as clerk so that Mrs. Kreuger could go upstairs and make supper for her family. Mr. Kreuger insisted they eat at five-thirty sharp, which did not leave his wife any time to rest from her day in the shop, but had she fixed supper much later, where would she have found the time she needed to wash and iron and scrub the linoleum floors and clean the bathroom, filthy after all the children and Mr. Kreuger himself had taken their baths?

"She worked herself to death," Alice Shepard would say of her mother. "I'm very fortuante to have a husband who takes care of me."

"My wife doesn't work," Bill Shepard liked to brag. "She stays home where she belongs. She knows her place."

"I love my house," Alice would say. "I spend a lot of time keeping it just so."

"Some women don't know when they have it good," Bill announced once. "The way they complain."

"It's just that sometimes," Alice Shepard mused, "you wonder what a different life would be like. That's all. You just wonder."

In 1954, when Lila was eleven, her mother conceived a second child.

"We should name him 'Dwight,' " Bill said. "After Ike."

"Dwight Shepard is a nice name," Alice said.

"It could be a girl baby," Lila said. "I could get a sister."

Her father reached across the supper table and mussed her hair. "I think we're due for a boy," he said. He winked at Lila and her mother. "Even things up around here, you know what I mean?"

In her fifth month, Alice started spotting. The doctor consigned her to bed for two weeks.

"We should have a talk, Lila," Alice said. Her eyes leaked tears. She was listening to "Stella Dallas" on the radio, and the bedroom seemed charged with intimate exchange. "About the facts."

"The facts?" Lila said, pretending not to understand.

"I started when I was your age. You could wake up

185

tomorrow and there it would be and you wouldn't know what it was."

"What what was?"

"The monthlies," her mother said. She hoisted herself up on her elbow, blew her nose, straightened the pillows behind her so she could lean against them as she sat. "You can turn my program off."

A man was saying, "Are you out of your mind, Amanda?" Lila snapped the knob to the left and silenced him. She pulled her mother's vanity chair to the side of the bed and sat down on its creweled seat.

"Now my mother never had this kind of talk with me," Alice said, "and I always told myself if I had a daughter, I wouldn't leave her ignorant, I wouldn't have her pick it up from others, hit or miss."

"Do you know what I remember most?" Lila told me. "Of everything she said that afternoon? That I should throw my soiled napkins in the outside trash can, not leave them in the wastebasket in the bathroom, because my father might smell them and it would make him sick. 'A man doesn't have the stomach for it,' she told me, and she believed it, she really did. Christ, my father hunted! He shot deer, he skinned rabbits. But menstrual blood would do him in. Well, I believed it too. For years. In the winter, at night, I would put my boots on and my jacket and carry a single Kotex, wrapped in tissues, to the garbage can beside the shed, and no one ever said 'Lila, this is crazy.' We were all caught up in it. It was an ancient thing."

An ancient thing. Generations of Chinese baby girls starved to death, or smothered, or drowned in rivers and wells. Jewish men thanking God each day "for not having made me a woman," this Old Testament deity who smote the Egyptians' first-born sons, daughters spared by their inconsequentiality. Muslim women shrouded in chadors, faces veiled, as if their bodies were wounds that had to be covered. In Salem, Massachusetts, women hung as witches.

186

"Some people call it 'the curse,'" Alice Shepard had told her daughter about menstruation. "I wouldn't go that far."

When Lila finished talking to me, I saw that she was cradling her womb, as if she had pain there, as if she were healing herself with her own hands.

In central Ohio, summer squalls are frequent, and sometimes tornadoes threaten the flat river towns. The weather bureau issues watches first, and then warnings when a funnel cloud is sighted, sirens from the local firehouse sounding the danger. People hurry to open their windows a crack, gather up the strongbox with the vital documents inside—deeds, policies, birth certificates, and wills—call in the dog, and herd themselves to their cellars, where they wait, sometimes for hours, for the all-clear siren to summon them upstairs again.

"There's a watch," Bill Shepard said. He had just come in from the foundry and was getting himself a glass of milk.

Lila was fixing supper—salmon patties and mashed potatoes, peas she had just shelled—and when she looked out the window, she saw the sky had yellowed like a bruise just beginning to show on the skin.

"Mom's upstairs," she said. "She didn't feel good again, so I'm cooking."

Thus they reported on their territories: his beyond the house, hers within.

"I'll look in on her," he said. "You call up when it's time to eat."

But before Lila could get the food on the table, the sirens cut through the wind-churned air and the Shepards had their dinner on the old kitchen table Alice kept in the cellar, beside her wringer washer, where she folded clothes in the winter that had dried overnight on the clotheslines she strung from the cold-water pipe to the hook driven into the cinderblock wall on the far side of the cellar. Bill Shepard had gotten out the oil lamps—"Nine times out of ten a wire goes down and we lose all our lights"—and he lit one even though the electricity was still intact. He set it in the center of the table, and when Lila brought the folding chairs from the storage room, the cellar was dark, except for the glowing kerosene lantern, its orange light fanned out across their plates and spilling over the table.

"Now Bill," Alice said. "Why would you—"

"Isn't this how the pioneers lived? They didn't—"

"We're not pioneers. It makes it scarier, Bill, it—"

"Scary?" He was taking the chairs from Lila and opening up each one. "Exciting, woman, exciting! When little Dwight's old enough, he'll appreciate a little excitement around here, I can tell you that."

Outside, the wind battered the house; tree branches split from limbs and rattled down the slate roof to the yard below. Somebody's cat had taken refuge under their porch, and they could hear the animal mewling like a baby cut off from its mother.

Lila said, "I bet that's Tabby," the Purdys' calico, part of the litter whose births Lila had watched the day she was helping old Mrs. Purdy take down her organdy curtains, because they needed to be washed. "Can't we bring her in?"

In the lamplight, her father's face broke into shifting planes, as if he were altering form. "Don't you hear those sirens?" he said. "Don't you know why we're down here to begin with?"

"She'll be fine, Lila," Alice said.

"Survival of the fittest," Bill said. "You might as well learn it while you're young."

Later, after the all-clear had sounded and the Shepards had taken their dishes upstairs, after Lila had cleaned the kitchen and coaxed Tabby from her hiding place with a leftover salmon patty and bowl of milk, after Alice had taken her bath and gotten into bed for the night, and Bill had read the sports section and Lila had finished two more chapters in *Little Women*, Alice Shepard screamed. By the time her husband got her to the hospital, she had dilated eight centimeters, and within an hour of her arrival, she delivered her second child, a boy, Dwight William Shepard, stillborn. If she had not been put to sleep with ether, Alice Shepard would have seen her son, unmoving and perfect, a tiny pale blue statue, a stone fertility god from a dead civilization.

"Nobody knows why these things happen," the doctor said. "They just do."

Alice Shepard would not conceive again. Perhaps the doctor advised against it. "At your age," he might have said, "the risks are just too great." Perhaps she told her husband, "If I lost another one, I don't think I could ever recover," or it might have been Bill Shepard's grief that shaped the future: "It's just not in the cards for me to have a son, that's all. It wasn't meant to be." Maybe they did try to have another child and failed, fear planted like a stone in Alice's womb, or loosed in Bill's semen, his sperm dying like poisoned fish.

"We have Lila," Alice said. "Why isn't that enough?"

"I don't know," he said. He raised his suffering face to hers. "I don't know."

If her father had avoided her before, now he seemed oblivious to Lila's presence. He retreated into grief as if it were a new room added on to the house, and though his body continued with the business of his life—work at the foundry, chores at home, hobbies he gradually took up again, occasional outings Alice managed to arrange—his spirit was now entirely absent, beyond Lila's reach, as lost to her as the brother buried in the cemetery two miles away. DWIGHT

189

WILLIAM SHEPARD, the granite marker read. JUNE 24, 1954. DIED AT BIRTH.

"I felt guilty for years," she told me. I watched her eyes travel back to Delaware, to the girl she had been, her own daughter now that age. "Once I dreamed I went to the cemetery and when I looked at the baby's stone, my own name was there; I was the one who was dead. I felt the greatest relief, looking at my own grave. As if I'd finally found the way to atone, to make it up to my father, to have his love."

She saw me looking at her with pity, that her imagination could have been so deranged.

"Listen," she said. "I'm not telling you all this for your sympathy. You had the same life, whether you know it yet or not. In one way or another, we were all taught to despise ourselves. Only the particulars differ."

3

Particulars:

In high school, she got good grades, especially in history and algebra. She belonged to the debating club. She joined the chorus, where she sang alto, and they came in second in statewide competitions held on the Antioch campus in Yellow Springs. She had friends. She was pretty. She enjoyed school dances, she had dates, and in her senior year she went steady for three months with Jim Meyerson, who planned to be a Presbyterian minister and always got her home by her curfew, if not before. *Lila Shepard*, the yearbook said: *Nicest smile.* After graduation, she worked her third summer in Beerman's Bakery, arriving at 6 A.M. to help Mr. Beerman bring the rolls and breads and pastries from the kitchen to the cases out front, and in the fall she enrolled as a freshman at Ohio State, where her roommate from Cincinnati taught Lila how to French-braid her shoulder-length brown hair.

"I don't believe you," Alice Shepard said to the social worker who called her from University Hospital the night Lila was admitted to the psychiatric ward. This was the end of her second semester, two weeks before final exams. "I saw her Sunday, and there's not a thing wrong with her. She's a good, normal American girl."

Lila had been in a hospital twice before: once to have her tonsils out at five, and once to see her mother after the stillbirth. "I can't wait to come home," her mother had wept, but Lila could remember thinking, I like it here. She thought it now, sitting on the edge of her bed in this plain and quiet room. She was eating her breakfast, which an aide had brought her on a tray. Orange juice and oatmeal, a glass of milk. "You can go to the dining room at the end of the hall when you feel stronger," the nurse had said. "Maybe in a few days."

"I don't want to feel stronger," Lila had said.

"Yes," said the nurse. "But you will."

Lila was just finishing her cereal when the doctor came to see her. He was a young man, thirty or so, with sandy hair and glasses. He was tall and slightly stooped, as if the doors in his house had been too low for him and he had learned to bend a bit in order not to bang his head. He seemed like a person who could adjust himself to any difficulty without complaining.

"So," he said. He sat on the chair beside her bed and crossed his legs, leaned back. He had her chart on his lap. He looked comfortable there, at home, as if he had sat like this many times before, and then it struck her that of course

191

he had, that patients came and went from this room like guests in a hotel and he visited them all with his promiscuous concern, his indiscriminate ease. "So. Your name is Lila, I see."

"Yes."

"I'm Dr. James, Lila. Why don't you sit back against your pillows and we'll talk for a few minutes. It says here that your boyfriend brought—"

"I don't have a boyfriend," she said.

"You don't."

"No."

"Who brought you to the hospital?"

"Oh," she said. She tried to see herself the night before, though time had turned to concrete, those hours miles long, a road she could hardly make out in the dark. Did she hear voices? C'mon, Lila, take off your clothes. They had driven to the far end of the campus, beyond the pastures of the agriculture school, out to the Olentangy River. He had taken a blanket out of the trunk, and a bottle of fruity wine. She remembered swigging some. Wasn't that the wine, in that plastic pitcher, next to her tissue box on the table she could wheel to her bed? The moon was nearly full, and its reflection floated like a huge luminous ball on the water. That's a homer, she told him. A what? A homer, she said. You're either drunk or crazy, that's the moon, he said. She watched him undress, folding his shirt and his slacks as if he were going to pack them in a suitcase, stuffing a sock into the toe of each shoe, carefully removing his watch and his high school ring. He grabbed the wine and swallowed, a rivulet running down his chin like blood from a tiny wound. When he took off his briefs, his moonlit nakedness stunned them both, and he ran away from her into the water, as if that had been his intention from the beginning. She could hear his feet breaking the river's luminous skin. C'mon, Lila, take off your clothes. What? Take off your clothes, it's warm in here. Her mother would have taken her by the hand and led her in, inch by inch. I'm scared, she called.

"What are you scared of, Lila?" the doctor said.

I'm scared, I'm scared, I'm scared!

C'mon, he said, all wet and bending over her now, pulling at her blouse, why do you think we came all the way out here, Lila? But she was trembling so badly, and making such a terrible sound in her throat, he thought she might be having convulsions. Will you stop it? he said. He dressed as fast as he could. Something's wrong with you, you're having a reaction to something, I'm taking you to emergency, he said, and he carried her like a stricken child to the car.

"Lila," the doctor was saying, "I want you to tell me if he hurt you in some way," but she was having trouble catching her breath, and making a terrible sound in her throat, and he gave her a shot of Thorazine and soon she was quiet again, almost asleep.

She would tell me, "He came at me with the whole Freudian shtick. A month of it. I bought it for years. Latent sexual longing for my father, hysterically transferred to this boy. All of this triggered by the water, which represented my mother. Blah, blah, blah."

"Then what was it?" I said. "What happened to you?"

"What happened to *you*?" Lila said, as if I, like her, had had a breakdown, or would, as if her terror were my own. "I told you: we all have the same life."

When the hospital released her, she spent a week in her parents' house. Her mother made pots of soup—lima bean, vegetable, fresh chicken stock—even though it was mid-June. "You're convalescing," Alice said, as if Lila were recovering from surgery, or a bout of pneumonia, or injuries suffered in an accident. "It will take you a while to get back your strength." She bought Lila vitamins and mineral oil and a new pair of slippers. "I'm going to build you up this summer so you'll be ready for school in the fall."

"I want your name cleared," Bill Shepard said. He slapped his palm, as if he were holding a document listing the crimes for which Lila had been mistakenly tried and convicted and jailed. "I'll hire a lawyer if I have to. I want it off your record."

By the end of August, Alice would say of Lila, "She's herself again," and her father would have given up his vendetta, and she herself would be able to sleep without using the pills the doctor had prescribed. She no longer dreamed, or else she no longer remembered dreaming. In the hospital, her nights had teemed with faces and voices and memories vivid as flame, so that waking was a rest toward which she struggled in the dark. Now the nightmares were gone, and that was a blessing, but what had become of the dreams in which she soared through clouds on her own wings and rode elephants over the tundra and flew after her father into the Scioto, where homers she had hit herself glowed like moons, rising, just beneath the surface?

4

"I went dead," Lila told me, speaking of the next seven years of her life, the frenzied, shouting sixties like mime to her, as if all that history our generation made could be reduced to a single street performer, waving his white-gloved hands in eccentric gesture, throwing his top hat to the sidewalk for coins.

She joined a sorority. She majored in education. She wore pleated skirts and knee socks and oxford-cloth button-down shirts whose collars and cuffs she stiffened with spray-on starch. If more and more girls her age were trading in their proper clothes for blue jeans and T-shirts and throwing away their rollers and giving up virginity as if it were an allergy they had finally outgrown, Lila did not seem to notice. "You look so young for your age," people told her, mistaking her ghostliness for a certain kind of health. Somewhere in that period she graduated from college, though she would tell me she did not remember the ceremony at all, and the next year she married, "a nice boy," she said, "from a good Republican family," who approved of her wardrobe and the manners her mother had taught her and the "sweet smile" she had learned to wear like an always-perfect wig, the kind that looks "so real" you hardly know it isn't. She taught fourth grade. She joined the Junior League and the Ladies' Auxiliary at the hospital where her husband was a resident. She would get pregnant during his last year of training, as they had planned. In the meantime, she studied French cooking. She took a course in Colonial antiques and scouted the Ohio countryside for sideboards and dry sinks and braided rugs. She read articles about "What Men Really Want": "security," one piece informed her, though another suggested "excitement—do something that surprises him every single day." It was as if she herself were in training, studying for the life she mimicked now. When the baby was three months old, Lila discovered that her husband was sleeping with a nurse at the hospital. "So I went to bed with my watercolor instructor. It seemed like what I was supposed to do. I didn't feel a thing. I didn't have the slightest idea yet how angry I was."

"Angry at your husband," I said, memories of my own marriage stirring.

She smiled ruefully, "Angry at history."

"You can't be angry at an abstraction."

"You think patriarchy is an abstraction?" she said. "You think chauvinism is an abstraction? Even the women who joined the Weathermen made the coffee, believe me. You think centuries of law making it illegal for women to be more than half alive are abstractions? I thought you used to work in civil rights." She took my hand in hers. "You're probably still looking for a man you can trust, aren't you?"

"Yes," I said, "I am."

She had tears in her eyes. "Maybe our daughters," she said. "But not us. We all have too much left to unlearn."

"Was it the affair?" I said. "Was that what—"

"Oh," she said. "You want the epiphany."

"Well—"

"You're going to turn me into one of your characters, aren't you? Another story about one poor woman whose husband turns out to be a jerk and her lover too, and then her temporary flight into feminist ideology. I'll be staring out the window in the last line, right, a sad old lady looking at the rain?"

"Lila—"

"It's okay, I forgive you, it's how you make a living." She winked and poured us both more tea.

The watercolor instructor and his wife were having a party for his students. It had rained for days, the lawn swampy, rose petals from their garden plastered to their flagstone walk. Lila came alone, her husband on call that night. "Drive carefully," he had told her; their marriage was still a loose weave of kindnesses. Soaked peonies bent to the ground and wind showered water from the trees. At the front door, she shook out her umbrella and rang the doorbell. The chimes rippled through the voices inside, a thin rivulet of bells. A child greeted her, ushered her into the front hall. She felt the warmth wrap like a robe around her rain-chilled body. She knew she should feel uncomfortable here, handing her coat to the child of her lover, but she could summon neither embarrassment nor fear. "If you don't come, I'll understand," he had told her, and she waited for anxiety to claim her now, but nothing that vivid stirred in Lila Shepard Frank. She was a wash of the palest tint on a white page. On a table, a bowl of willows under a Japanese woodcut. Grass cloth on the walls, an oriental runner stretching up the stairs. She had never been here before, and she took in these details as if they were elements in a scene she might paint. "You don't have talent," the teacher had said, "but you make interesting mistakes." She could imagine her own shadowy form in the background.

In the living room, faces she knew smiled at strangers, cigarette smoke thickening the common air. Conversations overlapped, half the words mangled, so that what she heard at the threshold was a pastiche of familiar sounds and foreign ones. This was always how she felt with people now: as if they spoke a language she only partially understood, though she feigned comprehension, pretended that she shared with them the meanings lost to her, the nuances numbness cancels out.

"I went dead," she would tell me, and the dead woman reached for the drink her host mixed for her at the butler's table crowded with bottles of liquor and Schweppes tonic and ginger ale.

"You have a lovely house," Lila said.

Behind them, cranes graced a hand-painted bamboo screen, the birds perfectly balanced, poised on single spindly legs.

He made himself a martini. "Don't you think this is kind of dangerous?" he said.

She could see he was not so much worried as exhilarated, the way he might look at the crest of a difficult ski

197

slope the moment before descent, or on a diving board's edge, his body imagining how it would rupture the air on its way to the water below. Her husband talked all the time about "close calls" at the hospital, and "near misses," and patients "hanging on by a hair." Sometimes she remembered her father the night they had huddled in the cellar during the tornado watch, the night her mother had gone into labor and lost the baby: "When little Dwight's old enough," her father had said, before the contractions had begun, "he'll appreciate a little excitement around here, I can tell you that." A few feet from where she stood now, a man was saying, "I think we ought to bomb them back to the Stone Age or get the hell out of there. A war's not a fucking tea party, for Christ's sake."

"Dangerous how?" Lila said to the watercolor instructor, whose fingers trembled against the sides of his martini glass. "I don't see—"

"Not now, Lila."

A woman was coming toward them, struggling to smile.

"Jane," he said, calling out to her as if she were not already approaching, as if he were trying to get the attention from her she had already trained like radar on them. "Come meet Lila Frank. She's been admiring the way we've decorated." He turned back to Lila. "This is my wife," he said. "My wife, Jane."

For a few moments the three of them chatted, and then he was gone—had he slipped behind the screen or down a trap door that had opened under his feet?—and Jane said, "Well, it was nice to meet you," her already-quiet voice a whisper now, as if the pleasantries had exhausted her. With what seemed like the last drop of energy she could summon, the watercolor instructor's wife extended her hand.

Lila looked at the lined palm, the long fingers, the polished nails as if she did not immediately recognize the gesture, did not know what was expected of her, and then, like a student of foreign cultures who quickly recalls the indigenous rituals, she slipped her own hand into Jane's. Warmth fled the woman's skin, and in her eyes Lila saw a look of the most profound and genuine terror. It was as if Jane were losing her own blood, as if Lila's handclasp were a siphon through which Jane's blood poured.

"It's nice to meet you too," Lila said, feeling faint, Jane's eyes still fastened on her, the woman dying, for a moment, in Lila's sight.

For a week, Jane's eyes imposed themselves like a scrim between Lila and everything else she looked at, that stricken gaze falling on food, on furniture, on the baby, on every other face she saw. "Are you all right?" people asked her, as if she, Lila, were the fear-struck woman. One morning she caught herself in the mirror—had she avoided her reflection all that time?—and the pain she saw there was her own, that white mask her own drained face, those suffering eyes Lila's now, tears she had re-fused to cry for years streaming unchecked down her cheeks.

"I don't know how I took care of the baby that day. I spent eight hours sobbing," Lila told me. "I thought my ribs would crack. I thought I was dying, but actually I was coming alive. That day was hard labor. November 17, 1971. I can't tell you what else was going on in the world, but that was the day I gave birth to myself. That was the day I was finally born."

She was twenty-eight years old. When she stopped crying, she looked out into History the way a refugee in steerage gazes over the ship's rail toward the far horizon, certain forms growing clearer, certain configurations suggesting realities she can name: building, harbor, lighthouse. We use the language we already have to define the world we have just discovered, words the bags we carry—suitcases, sacks, steamer trunks—from one life into another.

Lila could use these words: birth, mother, daughter, friend.

She walked each like a bridge whose structure she trusted, whose span took her into territory to which she felt summoned, as if by sisters already settled there, who had made the journey before her and welcomed her into their quarters: here is a chair, a bed, a cup of tea.

She read.

She dreamed.

"What's happening to you?" her husband said. "You don't make sense anymore."

One night a week she met with eight other women who, like her, were not making sense anymore, and together they parsed out a new grammar. "It was like being in an English class for the foreign-born," she told me. "The way we stammered. The disorientation." She grinned. "It was wonderful, wonderful!"

Birth. Mother. Daughter. Friend. A woman's etymology, a map the tongue could trace, the geography of gender, "female" a continent old as time.

"I guess I forgot you're a girl," her father had said.

She was remembering.

"It's a very important word," Lila told me. " 'Remember.' To restore what was amputated."

"Your past," I said, thinking of the way my stories existed only in the present, artful compendiums of the moment, characters surviving like amnesiacs the sudden lives which they had invented for themselves. Thinking of what I myself could not retrieve, that psychic sludge in which my own first years were mired.

"Ours," she said. "All of ours. The history of half the world."

She wanted me to go to meetings with her, and marches, and retreats for women she organized through a church

200

that had some property on Kelley's Island in Lake Erie. She wanted me to run for Congress. "You used to be in politics," she said. "You know all about campaigning. I think you'd be great." She wanted me to write a biography of Mother Jones.

I turned down every suggestion. "I've become a very private person," I told her. "I spend a lot of time alone."

After a while, we accepted each other as we were. I would call her when I'd seen her on television; once I bailed her out of jail—she had been arrested with a group of welfare mothers who had occupied the office of the County Executive. When she saw my stories in magazines, Lila sent notes she signed *Your fan*, and sometimes she'd mail me books she thought I'd like—diaries of farm women, feminist poetry.

Once a month we would take our daughters to lunch with us. "You were each other's first friends," we told the girls. "You're practically twins."

The children rolled their eyes at the romance their mothers had made of their births. Of course they were right to be skeptical. It was not their bond Lila and I recognized, celebrated, nutured with ritual: it was our own.

"I'm talked out," Lila said one afternoon. She was making bread, sprinkling flour over the mound of dough, then working it with her fingers and the heels of her hands. "Your turn."

I started to tell her about an art exhibit I'd been to the week before, tiny acrylic figures, vaguely human, in the corners of vast white canvases.

"What I'd really like to hear about is your childhood," she said. "Where were you born? What was your house like? I know you're Jewish, but you've never talked about that. Is it important to you? I don't know any of that stuff about you."

"I'm sketchy about an awful lot," I said, though lately

I had been having dreams, disquieting, still vivid when I woke, a maze of forgotten rooms through which I drifted, a faded brocade sofa suddenly familiar, window shades edged with fringe whose silky strands my fingers knew like my own hair, and down a distant hall voices I recognized, my name the summons they sang, the light growing dark, and still I could not find the room where they waited for me. "I don't have your kind of recall."

"You can learn," she said. "I can teach you."

"Oh, I don't—"

"I know it can be painful." She placed the dough in a glass bowl, covered it with cheesecloth.

"I just don't think I need—"

"To know who you are? That's not exactly a peripheral activity. What kind of writer can you be, what kind of mother?"

"Now listen, Lila, I don't have to be exactly like you." My eyes stung, and I turned away from her, embarrassed.

"I'm sorry," she said. "I can be disgustingly pushy." She was at the sink now, washing her hands, her back to me as if to give me the privacy I needed to cope with my unexpected tears. "It's just that I don't think that anyone who listens as well as you do to someone else's story isn't ready to know her own."

"I don't know how," I said, and it seemed as if a breath I had been holding for years had just been released, some natural function restored, the life-serving rhythm, long arrested, beginning again.

"Well, you start by relaxing," she said, coming to stand behind me. She massaged my scalp for me, and temples, and the tense cords of my neck. She lulled me close to sleep.

"What's your first memory?" she said, "That's a good way to start."

"I don't—"

202

"Let it rise," she whispered. "Let it come to the surface."

The sudden smell of loam.

"Morning glories." My heart contracted, as if tangled in vines. Purple blossoms exploded on Lila's kitchen wall. I covered my eyes with my hands.

"How old are you?" She pulled her chair close to mine, stroked my hair as if I were a child.

"Two," I said. "Maybe younger." Years fell from my voice.

"Where are you? In a garden?"

I opened my eyes to the trellised blooms. "On the porch." My grandfather knelt in front of the wooden planter he had built. Filtered through the floor-to-ceiling screens, the sun's light shimmered on the curve of his back, his white hair shone, a radiant hand rose: he was watering his flowers.

"Is anyone with you?"

But I was already lifting up out of my chair, my legs wobbly as a baby's just beginning to walk, and his name, unspoken for years, was a primal cry on my tongue: "Pa. Pa. Pa." I could have clawed through Lila's wall to the thin air outside if she had not been there to claim me back to the present.

That night I called my mother in Pittsburgh. "Was I close to your father," I asked her, "when we lived in Boston?" Naming the place hurt me now, the numbness rupturing. "Was I—"

"Close?" she said, and she sounded exhausted, as if she had been waiting all these years for us to have this conversation, as if she had had to keep herself ready for my questions for decades and the effort had depleted her, almost worn her out. She sighed. "Close isn't the word for it." Her voice broke. "He lived for you, don't you remember? He lived for you."

5

When she was forty, a doctor discovered a tumor growing in the lining of Lila Frank's heart. "Inoperable," she told me the day she learned. "Shit."

Birth, mother, daughter, friend. Add "death" to the language she had learned to speak.

"Help me write the service," she said. "You're the word woman."

After her death, her child would live with her father and his second wife. Lila was friends with both of them— "I taught him a lot," she would say of her ex-husband— and the day after the diagnosis, she told her daughter, "I think you should move in with your father now. You can visit me all the time, but I'm going to be pretty sick off and on and it's going to be very hard on you."

"I'll let you know when I'm overwhelmed, Mom," her twelve-year-old said, and she laid her head against her mother's chest, Lila's still-strong heart beating against her daughter's cheek.

Lila lived for another year, and each day her daughter coiled her gangly height upon her mother's lap and they sang a lullaby together that Lila had crooned years ago to the baby whose birth I had shared. When the morphine claimed her memory, and the lyrics were lost to her, Lila's child sang alone, holding her mother's jaundiced hand.

In the last months, the Shepards came from Delaware, two elderly people now, beyond the shocks their daughter's life would offer them. She was theirs and they loved her. They took over a bedroom in the group house where Lila and her daughter still resided, at least two of the women there openly lovers. "Live and let live," Alice Shepard said to me and then that inadvertently uttered prayer bowed her for a moment, her whole body loosened by the plea, and her knees buckled. I helped her sit down. "Bill is so torn up," she said. "I don't think he ever knew how close he was to Lila. Do you think that can be? Love a secret you keep from yourself?"

I said I thought that could happen, and often did.

"Well," she said, "at least he knows it now." Forty years traveled in her eyes, a swirling river of memory, a sudden flood.

For Lila, time collapsed entirely. If she had become intense, her last decade as passionate as the one before it had been dimmed—"I went dead," she had told me and how the irony wounded now—in these final months she shone like a moon whose radiance comes from a source beyond itself, unchronicled light, vaster than the tiny grids of calendars could possibly contain.

She lost her hair. I took her to buy a wig at a costume store an actress friend had suggested to us, the owner a woman "who will get you anything you want." Lila chose waist-length black tresses she plaited into the French braid her college roommate had taught her how to do years before, whatever years were now.

Her weight dropped. Her energy failed her. Speech itself became an effort she could not sustain. Only the shining maintained itself, and it seemed that her body was removing itself, pound by pound, function by function, so that the light she was becoming could finally assert its claim: I am Lila Shepard Frank.

She was dreaming when she died. We could see that flickering behind her closed eyes, and tremors suggesting movement in another realm. Once she made a sound, guttural and raw, and though others in the room with her took it as the rattle of death, I knew she was dreaming her daughter's birth, that throaty call the one I'd heard her make during that other labor, years before, whatever years are now.

6

The world is always giving birth to itself, History's contractions a perpetual labor, our lives her blood-swaddled brood. Who isn't always a newborn, every word we utter and write down the single cry we make with the single breath we draw? Pa, Flo, Daniel, Susan, Lila—in dreams I follow them out of time, as if we were birds migrating to a warmer place, or fish swimming together through the unmappable depths of the sea. I wake consoled, take up again my moment here, others I love and will come to love waiting for me in the early morning light.